MW00474400

Keynotes in Criminology and Criminal Justice

RACE, CRIME, AND JUSTICE: THE CONTINUING AMERICAN DILEMMA

Steven E. Barkan

University of Maine

New York   Oxford
OXFORD UNIVERSITY PRESS

Oxford University Press is a department of the University of Oxford.
It furthers the University's objective of excellence in research, scholarship,
and education by publishing worldwide. Oxford is a registered trade mark of
Oxford University Press in the UK and certain other countries.

Published in the United States of America by Oxford University Press
198 Madison Avenue, New York, NY 10016, United States of America.

For titles covered by Section 112 of the US Higher Education
Opportunity Act, please visit www.oup.com/us/he for the latest
information about pricing and alternate formats.

Library of Congress Cataloging-in-Publication Data

Names: Barkan, Steven E., 1951- author.
Title: Race, crime, and justice : the continuing American dilemma /
  Steven E. Barkan.
Description: 1st Edition. | New York : Oxford University Press, [2018] |
  Series: Keynotes in criminology and criminal justice | Includes index.
Identifiers: LCCN 2018006685 (print) | LCCN 2018018424 (ebook) |
  ISBN 9780190647285 (eBook) | ISBN 9780190272548 (pbk. : alk. paper)
Subjects: LCSH: Crime and race—United States. | Discrimination in criminal
  justice administration—United States.
Classification: LCC HV6197.U5 (ebook) | LCC HV6197.U5 B37 2018 (print) |
  DDC 364.08/00973—dc23
LC record available at https://lccn.loc.gov/2018006685

9 8 7 6 5 4 3 2 1
Printed by Sheridan Books, Inc., United States of America

CONTENTS

ACKNOWLEDGMENTS

I wish to thank several people who helped bring this book to frui-
tion. Steve Helba and Henry Pontell showed great faith in my ability
to write the book, and I am grateful for their support since the beginning of this project. The Oxford University Press production staff ef-
fectively and efficiently brought my manuscript to publication; I owe
all these people who work behind the scenes an enormous debt, as does
every book author. I also owe an enormous debt to the many reviewers
who provided very helpful suggestions on earlier versions of the manuscript. I adopted many of their suggestions while not incorporating
other ideas for lack of space. Any flaws that might remain in the book,
of course, are mine alone. These reviewers were Tim Berard (Kent
State University), Jean Dawson (Franklin Pierce University), S. Marlon
Gayadeen (SUNY Buffalo State), Addrain Conyers (Marist College),
Ebony L. Johnson (The University of Alabama), Elyshia D. Aseltine
(Towson University), Thomas S. Alexander (University of Maryland-
College Park [Shady Grove campus]), Gail F. Beaudoin (University of
Massachusetts Lowell), Francis M. Williams (Plymouth State University),
Sandra Lee Browning (University of Cincinnati), Janice Anne Iwama
(University of Massachusetts Boston), Robbin Day Brooks (Arizona State
University), Tim Robicheaux (The Pennsylvania State University), Lee E.
Ross (University of Central Florida), and Peter R. Grahame (Pennsylvania
State University).

As in all my books, I thank Barbara Tennent and David and Joel
Barkan, who have supported me through many years of textbook writing
and far too many defeats of our favored electoral candidates and favorite

sports teams. The birth of my first grandchild, Avery, as I was finishing this book brought great joy to her parents and grandparents, who fervently hope that the future holds great promise for her personally and for our nation and world as a whole. My final thanks go as always to my late parents, Morry and Sylvia Barkan, who would have cherished the day when a book like this would not need to be written.

Keynotes in Criminology and Criminal Justice Series

This Series is designed to provide essential knowledge on important contemporary matters of crime, law, and justice to a broad audience of readers including students, educators, researchers, and practitioners alike, and in a format that is not only authoritative, but highly engaging and concise. Nationally and internationally respected scholars share their knowledge and unique insights in comprehensive surveys and penetrating analyses of a variety of major contemporary issues central to the study of criminology, criminal justice, and social justice more generally. Keynotes Series books cover such areas as electronic crime, race, crime and justice, white-collar and corporate crime, violence in international perspective, gender and crime, gangs, mass incarceration, and financial fraud.

I invite you to examine the Series and see how these readable, affordable, topical, and highly informative books can be used to help educate a new generation of students in understanding the social realities surrounding crime and justice in both domestic and global perspective.

Henry N. Pontell, Editor
Keynotes in Criminology and Criminal Justice Series
Distinguished Professor, John Jay College of Criminal Justice of The City University of New York
Professor Emeritus, University of California, Irvine

ABOUT THE AUTHOR

Steven E. Barkan is professor of sociology at the University of Maine. He is past president of the Society for the Study of Social Problems and of the Textbook and Academic Authors Association. Professor Barkan welcomes comments on this book at barkan@maine.edu.

PREFACE

This brief book discusses many aspects of race, crime, and criminal justice in the United States. The disproportionate involvement of African Americans, Latinos, and Native Americans in the criminal justice system is one of the central issues of our time. As mass incarceration swept the nation during the last few decades, members of these three groups were swept up into jails and prisons far beyond their share of the national population. This book examines why this happened, along with many other issues regarding the racialization of crime and justice. Because most research on these issues compares African Americans with non-Latino whites, much of our discussion will do the same. Thankfully, a growing amount of research involves Latinos and, to a smaller extent, Native Americans and Asian Americans, and we will discuss this research when possible.

Chapter 1 examines racial/ethnic disparities in criminal justice involvement and the rise and collateral consequences of mass incarceration. Chapter 2 discusses racial bias in news media coverage of crime and racial differences in public opinion on crime and justice. Chapter 3 addresses the controversial issue of racial/ethnic differences in rates of criminal behavior, while Chapter 4 reviews similar differences in criminal victimization. The book then turns to the fundamental issues of racial/ethnic disparities and discrimination in policing (Chapter 5) and prosecution and sentencing (Chapter 6). Chapter 7, the final chapter, summarizes the book's discussion and outlines social and criminal justice policies that, if successfully implemented, would help relieve the many problems the book discusses.

By the end of the book, readers should have a new appreciation and broad understanding of the key issues and evidence concerning race, crime, and criminal justice in the United States today. Because racial/ethnic disparities in crime and justice continue to stain the American dream, it is important for all Americans to recognize these disparities and for public policy and civic activism to do everything possible to reduce them and, if we may dream, to eliminate them.

[1]

RACE, CRIME, AND JUSTICE IN AMERICAN SOCIETY

Chapter Outline

Learning Questions

1. What is meant by racial disparities?
2. What are the imprisonment rates by race and ethnicity?
3. Why did the United States undertake the get-tough approach?
4. How and why has the legal war on drugs disproportionately affected people of color?
5. What are the major collateral consequences of mass incarceration?

We regularly hear about police shootings of young African American men who were unarmed, or probably so. Young African Americans and Latinos repeatedly report being hassled by police for merely walking down the street or standing around talking. Our nation's jails and prisons are flooded with African Americans and Latinos, most of them young males. In many urban neighborhoods, an arrest and prison record has become almost the norm rather than the exception. Many children of color have a parent behind bars, often for offenses that would not merit incarceration in other democracies.

How did the United States arrive reach this alarming state of affairs? What are the racial dimensions of crime and justice in America? What can be done to reduce the racialization of crime and justice? This brief book tries to answer these questions by shedding some light on one of the most urgent issues of the modern era. We begin our discussion by recalling the past.

THE CONTINUING AMERICAN DILEMMA

This book's subtitle, "The Continuing American Dilemma," comes from Gunnar Myrdal's powerful 1944 study, *An American Dilemma: The Negro Problem and Modern Democracy* (Myrdal 1944). The Carnegie Corporation of New York had asked Myrdal, a Swedish social scientist, to investigate racial inequality and race relations in the United States, with a focus on African Americans (who were then widely called Negroes); *An American Dilemma* was his report of his findings. In chapter after chapter spanning almost 1,500 pages, Myrdal spelled out the history and extent of racial prejudice, racial discrimination, and racial inequality in the United

States. In doing so, he squarely blamed the higher levels of poverty and other problems facing African Americans on the prejudice and inequality they encountered from birth through adulthood.

Two decades after Myrdal's report, President Lyndon Johnson established a commission in 1965 to examine the growing crime problem in America. Two years later, this commission's final report blamed urban residents' higher crime rates on the many negative social conditions in which they lived. "Crime flourishes, and always has flourished," the report declared, "in city slums, those neighborhoods where overcrowding, economic deprivation, social disruption and racial discrimination are endemic" (President's Commission on Law Enforcement and Administration of Justice 1967:17).

President Johnson also established a commission to examine the causes of the urban riots of the 1960s. This commission's final report attributed the riots to the history of racism and racial inequality in the United States. It declared its "basic conclusion" in a searing passage that became famous: "Our nation is moving toward two societies, one black, one white—separate and unequal." It added, "Discrimination and segregation have long permeated much of American life; they now threaten the future of every American. . . . Race prejudice has shaped our history decisively; it now threatens to affect our future. White racism is essentially responsible for the explosive mixture which has been accumulating in our cities since the end of World War II" (Kerner Commission 1968:1–2).

It is now a half century since these two presidential commission reports and about 75 years since Myrdal's report. How much has changed during these many decades? As the old saying goes, the more things change, the more they stay the same.

It is true that legal racial segregation ended by the mid-1960s and that African Americans and other people of color have made gains in political, economic, and social life that would have been unimaginable back then. Yet it is also true that the United States continues to be filled with racial prejudice, illegal racial discrimination, and racial inequality. In particular, African Americans, Latinos, and Native Americans continue to be much poorer than non-Latino whites, to reside in areas with substandard living conditions, to lack educational and employment opportunities, and to be victims of hate crimes and everyday racial slights (Andersen 2018; Bonilla-Silva 2018).

We lack the space to document this continuing racial inequality, but suffice it to say that the United States continues to have separate and sorely unequal societies based on race and ethnicity, and that the racial prejudice and discriminatory practices of white individuals and of organizations and institutions controlled by whites account for the racial inequality that continues to stain the American dream (Feagin 2014; Wallis 2017). More than a century ago, the great African American scholar W. E. B. Du Bois (1903:vii) wrote, "The problem of the Twentieth Century is the problem of the color line." A mountain of social science evidence shows that the color line remains a paramount problem of our current century.

DEFINING SOME CONCEPTS

Before proceeding further, we should define and discuss several concepts that appear in this chapter and throughout the book. Readers are encouraged to consult the many books about race and ethnicity in America for a much fuller discussion of these concepts.

Race and Ethnicity

Two basic but complex concepts are *race* and *ethnicity*. **Race** refers to a category of people who share certain inherited physical traits, including skin tone and facial features. Although the various races as they are commonly conceived differ in physical appearance, social scientists emphasize that race is much more of social concept than a biological concept (Andersen 2018; Smedley and Smedley 2012). Several reasons underlie this emphasis.

First, sometimes there are more physical differences within a race than between races: Some people we call "white" have rather dark skin, while others have lighter skin; some people we call "black" have dark skin, while others have lighter skin. Because so much interracial reproduction has occurred in the United States and elsewhere since the days of slavery, any clear differences among the races that might have existed hundreds of thousands of years ago no longer exist.

Second, someone's race designation is often arbitrary. President Barack Obama had an African father and a white mother. In terms of his ancestry, he was half black and half white, yet he identifies as African American, and the public agrees that he is an African American If someone has a white parent and another parent who is the child of a black parent and white parent, American society would likely regard this person as black, even though this person's ancestry is 75% white. However, many Latin American nations would deem this person to be white.

Third, less than 0.1% of all DNA in human bodies accounts for the physical differences that lead us to categorize people into different races (Begley 2008). Biologically speaking, then, the races are much more similar than different.

All these considerations lead race scholars to regard race as a *social construction*, meaning that race is a concept that has no objective reality but exists only because our society had decided that it should exist. In turn, many social scientists prefer to use the term *ethnicity* instead of race when discussing social categories of people with certain cultural and other characteristics. **Ethnicity**, then, refers to a subgroup of the population with shared social, cultural, and historical experiences. What we usually call *races* are in fact ethnic groups. Scholarly research still commonly uses the term *race* when discussing African Americans, Asians, Native Americans, and whites, with Latinos considered an ethnic group rather than a race; this book follows this practice.

Racial Prejudice and Racial Stereotypes

Two additional terms worth discussing are *racial prejudice* and racial and ethnic *stereotypes*. **Racial prejudice** (also *ethnic prejudice*) refers to negative attitudes and perceptions about social categories of people because of their perceived race or ethnicity. Meanwhile, **racial stereotypes** (also *ethnic stereotypes*) refer to false or simplified generalizations about people because of their race or ethnicity. Prejudice contributes to stereo-typing, and stereotypes contribute to prejudice (Andersen 2018).

Racial Discrimination

A final term is **racial discrimination** (also *ethnic discrimination*), which refers to harsher treatment and/or the denial of rights and opportunities because of someone's race or ethnicity. This discrimination may occur at the *individual* level, as when someone is not hired because of her/his race or ethnicity, and it also may occur at the *institutional* level, when discrimi-nation characterizes the practices of whole institutions such as education, housing, and law enforcement. As Chapters 5 and 6 will emphasize, racial discrimination may occur even when the individuals and institutions practicing it are not consciously intending it.

RACE AND CRIMINAL JUSTICE INVOLVEMENT

In regard to crime and criminal justice, we will see ample evidence of racial discrimination in the pages that follow. As the chapter titles of this book suggest, the interplay of race, crime, and criminal justice involves many dimensions: public opinion, criminal behavior and victimization, and the operation of the many phases of the criminal justice system. To provide a backdrop for the later discussion of these dimensions, this first chapter discusses a harsh reality of U.S. criminal justice: racial disparities in criminal justice involvement.

Here again, we need to define some terms. Let's start with **criminal justice involvement**, which commonly refers to experiencing one or more of the following official legal sanctions: (1) arrest, (2) conviction, and (3) sentencing, especially incarceration in prison or jail. Police also stop, question, and sometimes search persons they regard as suspicious, without an arrest occurring. Though certainly serious for the persons stopped, this experience does not involve an official sanction and thus is not considered a dimension of criminal justice involvement as scholars usually use this term. Meanwhile, **racial disparities** refers to outcomes that affect one race/ethnicity more than another race/ethnicity. In regard to criminal justice involvement, the term refers to the greater likelihood of people of color of being arrested, convicted, and/or incarcerated.

Our discussion of these disparities will now focus on incarceration, which provides the most striking evidence of these disparities. As this chapter discusses later, the United States has followed a policy of **mass incarceration** since the 1970s, characterized by longer and more certain prison terms for people convicted of **conventional crime** (e.g., violent crime, property crime, drug offenses; also called *street crime*). This policy quadrupled the number of prison inmates and also greatly increased the size of the **correctional population** (the number of people in prison or jail or on probation or parole). These changes fell more heavily upon African Americans and, to a smaller extent, Latinos than other racial/ethnic groups. As the imprisonment rate surged, so did the number of African American and Latino prisoners.

This phenomenon shocked Ernie Preate, Jr.. When he was a hard-nosed prosecutor before becoming Pennsylvania's state attorney general, Preate sought harsh sentences for convicted criminals. Ironically, he later spent time in prison after pleading guilty to charges of accepting illegal campaign contributions. There he quickly noticed many African Americans serving long prison terms for minor drug offenses. "I'll never forget it," he later recalled. "In January of 1996, I walked into the mess hall the first night I was [in prison], and I turned around and I said, 'Oh, my God, what have we created?' It was a sea of black and brown faces" (Bleyer 2001:28).

Imprisonment

This sea of black and brown faces still exists. At year-end 2016, the most recent available data at the time of this writing, U.S. state and federal prisons held about 1.5 million sentenced persons. African Americans comprised about 33% of these prisoners, Latinos 23%, and non-Latino whites 30% (Carson 2018). (A side note: Because many states classify Latino prisoners as white, Latinos likely comprise a higher percentage of prisoners, and non-Latino whites a lower percentage, than just indicated.) To put prisoners' racial/ethnic com-position into context, keep in mind that in 2016 African Americans comprised about 13% of the entire U.S. population, Latinos 18%, and non-Latino whites 61% (U.S. Census Bureau 2017).

Let's now compare the numbers in the preceding paragraph. This comparison yields three conclusions:

- African Americans comprise 33% of all prisoners, although they account for only 13% of the U.S. population.
- Latinos comprise 23% of all prisoners (and likely a higher percentage), although they account for only 18% of the U.S. population.
- Non-Latino whites comprise only 30% of all prisoners (and likely a lower percentage), although they account for 61% of the U.S. population.

The first conclusion demonstrates a striking disparity, with the percentage of African American prisoners 2.5 times greater than the percentage of African Americans nationwide. The second conclusion shows a smaller disparity, with the percentage of Latino prisoners 1.3 times higher higher than the percentage of Latinos nationwide. Meanwhile, the percentage of non-Latino white prisoners is only half the percentage of non-Latino whites nationwide.

Another common measure of racial disparities in imprisonment involves dividing the number of prisoners in each racial/ethnic group by the group's national population, and then multiplying by 100,000 to yield an imprisonment rate per 100,000 population. This calculation yields the following rates per population 18 and older (Carson 2018):

- African Americans: 1,608 prisoners per 100,000 population 18 and older
- Latinos: 856 prisoners per 100,000 population 18 and older
- Non-Latino whites: 274 prisoners per 100,000 population 18 and older

These rates again tell a compelling story of racial disparities in imprisonment. The African American imprisonment rate is almost six times higher than the non-Latino white rate, while the Latino rate is 3.1 times higher

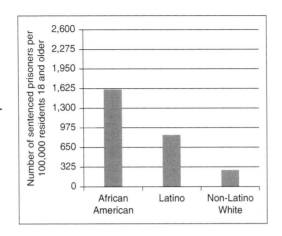

FIGURE 1.1 | Race/Ethnicity and Rates of Imprisonment, United States, 2016
Source: Carson 2017.

than the non-Latino white rate. Figure 1.1 depicts these large racial/ethnic disparities in incarceration. In some states, the African American imprisonment rate is more than ten times higher than the white rate (Nellis 2016).

Jail Inmates

So far we have presented data on prisoners. Incarceration in prisons is generally reserved for individuals convicted of a **felony**, a crime for which the possible incarceration is at least one year. Many more people get arrested for a **misdemeanor**, a crime for which the possible incarceration is less than one year. People convicted of misdemeanors who are incarcerated almost always go to a local or county jail rather than to a state or federal prison. Many people also spend time in jail awaiting court hearings and the disposition of their cases. It is therefore also instructive to consider racial/ethnic disparities in the jail population.

At midyear 2016, U.S. county and local jails held almost 705,000 jail inmates. Of this number, about 35% were African American, 15% Latino, and 48% non-Latino white (Zeng 2018). Because the African American share of jail inmates was nearly identical to the share of prison inmates, the African American percentage of jail inmates was again about 2.5 times higher than the African American share of the national population. At the same time, the percentage of jail inmates who were Latino was a bit lower than the Latino percentage nationwide (but keep in mind that many Latino jail inmates are also classified as white). We can again report the incarceration rate by race/ethnic group for jail inmates, with data existing this time for Asians and for Native Americans:

- African Americans: 599 jail inmates per 100,000 population
- Asians and Pacific Islanders   30 jail inmates per 100,000 population
- Latinos: 185 jail inmates per 100,000 population
- Native Americans: 359 jail inmates per 100,000 population
- Non-Latino whites: 171 jail inmates per 100,000 population

Although the Latino jail inmate rate is only slightly higher than the non-Latino white rate, the African American rate is 3.5 times higher than that rate. The Native American rate is twice as higher as the non-Latino white rate, while the Asian and Pacific Islander rate is a minuscule 30 jail inmates per 100,000.

The Correctional Population

In addition to or instead of incarceration, convicted defendants may be put on probation, and released inmates may be put on parole. As noted earlier, the total number of people in prison or jail or on probation or parole comprises the *correctional population*. In 2015, the latest year of available data at the time of this writing, more than 6.8 million Americans were in the correctional population (Kaeble and Glaze 2016). Of this number, about 28% were African Americans (Bureau of Justice

Statistics 2018). The total correctional supervision rates per 100,000 population were as follows:

- African Americans: 4,648 under correctional supervision per 100,000
- Latinos: 1,562 under correctional supervision per 100,000
- Non-Latino whites: 1,328 under correctional supervision per 100,000

Here again is clear evidence of racial disparity, with African Americans 3.5 times more likely than non-Latino whites to be under correctional supervision. In other evidence of racial disparities, a staggering one-third of African American men have a felony conviction, compared to just 13% of all adult men (2010 data); 15% of African American men have been in prison, compared to just 6% of all adult men (Shannon et al. 2017). Some estimates suggest that one-fourth of African American males born today can expect to go to prison (Kessler 2015). Reflecting this dire situation, a National Research Council report (Travis, Western, and Redburn 2014:13–14) found that "African American men born since the late 1960s are more likely to have served time in prison than to have completed college with a 4-year degree. And African American men under age 35 who failed to finish high school are now more likely to be behind bars than employed in the labor market."

A Critical Question

All of these numbers show strong evidence of racial/ethnic disparity in criminal justice involvement. African Americans and Native Americans (judging from jail inmates) are the most heavily incarcerated, with Latinos following behind. At the other end of spectrum, Asians are hardly involved at all (again judging from jail inmates) compared to the other racial/ethnic groups, with non-Latino whites in between.

A critical question is this: Exactly why do these disparities exist? Do they reflect disparities in conventional criminal behavior—that is, actual greater criminality by some racial/ethnic groups compared to others (the *differential involvement in criminal behavior thesis*)? Do they instead reflect racial/ethnic bias, however unconscious, by police, prosecutors, and other criminal justice professionals, and their targeting of behaviors committed by people of color and of neighborhoods populated by people of color (the *differential enforcement thesis* or *biased criminal justice system thesis*)? Do racial/ethnic disparities in criminal justice involvement reflect a combination of these dynamics?

Fortunately, criminologists have tried to answer these questions. Drawing on their research, a quick answer is that all of the dynamics just listed matter. America's racial/ethnic groups do appear to commit serious conventional crime at different rates; racial/ethnic bias by criminal justice professionals does appear to exist; and some criminal justice policies target, intentionally or not, some racial/ethnic groups more than others (Piquero, Piquero, and Stewart 2015). As criminologist Robert D. Crutchfield and retired judge Gregory A. Weeks (2015) observe, "There is overrepresentation of minority group members among those engaging in crime, but even after this is taken into account, people of color are overrepresented in U.S. prisons and jails." Later chapters of this book provide evidence of all the dynamics producing racial/ethnic disparities in criminal justice involvement.

Two Additional Facts to Keep in Mind

As we consider racial disparities in criminal justice involvement, it is important to keep two additional facts in mind.

The first fact is that most African Americans, Latinos, and Native Americans definitely do *not* commit crime. Even if certain racial/ethnic groups in the United States do have higher crime rates than other groups, almost all of the people in the apparent "crime-prone" groups still do *not* commit crime. To the extent that racial/ethnic differences in serious crime exist, they reflect the behavior of a very small group of offenders rather than that of people of color more generally (Agnew 2016).

The second fact to remember concerns **white-collar crime**. White-collar criminals such as corporate executives who market unsafe products or dump toxic waste into rivers rarely get arrested, even though the economic and human toll of white-collar crime far exceeds that of conventional crime (Reiman and Leighton 2017). Because whites dominate the ranks of corporate executives and other white-collar occupations, almost all white-collar criminals are white. Even if some people of color, then, commit more than their fair share of conventional crime, whites hold the monopoly on unforgivable white-collar crime.

HOW WE GOT WHERE WE ARE

How did we arrive at the situation documented in the preceding pages? Why are so many people of color behind bars? Why did mass incarceration arise? The following brief summary draws on several accounts of the rise of mass incarceration (Alexander 2012; Beckett and Sasson 2004; Fortner 2015; Gottschalk 2006; Hinton 2016; Pfaff 2017).

The Get-Tough Approach and Mass Incarceration

Between the 1930s and the early 1970s, the U.S. incarceration rate was fairly stable and slightly higher than average among all Western nations (the United States, Canada, and Western Europe) (Tonry 2008). It then soared after the early 1970s before leveling off about a decade ago and then declining slightly in recent years. Even so, the imprisonment rate, which was only 93 prisoners per 100,000 population and 196,000 inmates in 1972, today stands at 450 prisoners per 100,000 and more than 1.5 million prisoners (2016 data) (Carson 2018). Today's rate is about five times higher than the 1972 rate, and the number of prisoners is almost eight times higher. Meanwhile, the cost of corrections for the state, federal, and local governments rose from $6.9 billion in 1980 to more than $80 billion a few years ago (Kyckelhahn 2015). Relatedly, the U.S. incarceration rate today for prison and jail inmates combined is also about seven times higher than the average rate for all Western democracies (Travis et al. 2014), and the United States spends much, much more money on corrections than do other democracies.

So why did incarceration rise so much for four decades after the early 1970s? At least three factors explain why mass incarceration developed: rising violent crime, changes in criminal justice policy, and racial prejudice.

Rising Violent Crime

The violent crime rate rose during the 1960s and well into the 1970s and early 1980s, in part because the post–World War II baby boom generation was reaching the high-crime age range: 15–30. Despite the increase in violent crime in the 1960s, the incarceration rate actually fell during that decade. As violent crime continued to rise during the 1970s, incarceration finally began rising as well. It continued to rise during the 1990s and into the last decade, even though conventional crime declined sharply after the early 1990s.

Thus, although concern over rising violent crime fueled the surge in incarceration that began in the early 1970s, it cannot be said that rising crime was the only reason for rising incarceration, because incarceration increased even when crime was falling. Incarceration also rose steadily during and after the 1970s even though public concern about crime as measured in national surveys remained stable after the mid-1970s and then dropped after the mid-1990s. These related trends led economist Steven Raphael (2009:91) to observe that "increases in crime cannot explain a substantial portion of incarceration growth." Sociologists Katherine Beckett and Theodore Sasson (2004:17) likewise conclude, "The massive expansion of the criminal justice system has not been primarily a consequence of rising levels of crime."

Changes in Criminal Justice Policy

If rising crime only partly explains rising incarceration, what other factors played a role? Here scholars emphasize the role played by criminal justice policy. To be more specific, beginning in the 1970s the United States adopted a "get-tough" approach to crime (Pfaff 2017). Legislatures imposed minimum and mandatory terms and increased the length of maximum terms; prosecutors became more stringent in their plea bargaining, leading more offenders to receive a prison sentence rather than a lighter sentence; and judges imposed longer prison sentences. These policy changes accounted mightily for the incarceration boom, especially during the period following the early 1990s when incarceration continued to soar even as crime was falling dramatically.

Racial Prejudice

It is fair to say that rising violent crime did create the initial motivation for the get-tough approach that led to mass incarceration, even if this approach persisted when crime was falling. But in addition to rising crime, racial fears also played a critical role, as concern about crime was heightened because politicians and the public saw black people committing violent crime. The urban riots of the 1960s scared whites throughout the nation, and African Americans were also apparently committing conventional violent crime disproportionately. These facts combined with deep-rooted racial prejudice against African Americans to fuel concern about crime and to lead to calls for harsher criminal sentencing (Alexander 2012).

Even though African American elected officials and citizens also urged a crackdown on crime to protect their communities (Fortner 2015), racial fears played a role in this crackdown. In the wake of the 1960s urban riots, President Lyndon Johnson called for a war on crime and expanded federal funding for local crime control efforts (Hinton 2016). Politicians in the Republican Party began speaking of crime in racially coded language to appeal to whites in the South and elsewhere who had hostile feelings about African Americans. Richard Nixon's 1968 presidential campaign explicitly appealed to whites by linking African Americans and violent crime. As Nixon aide John Ehrlichman later wrote of this campaign, "We'll go after the racists. That subliminal appeal to the anti-African-American voter was always present in Nixon's statements and speeches" (quoted in Beckett and Sasson, 2004:54). Ronald Regan's 1980 presidential campaign also featured the Republican Party's emphasis on "law and order."

The Legal War on Drugs

The Nixon White House initiated the war on drugs in the early 1970s. One goal of this effort was to increase public hostility toward antiwar protesters and African Americans. John Ehrlichman, later recalled, "By getting the public to associate the hippies with marijuana and blacks with heroin, and then criminalizing both heavily, we could disrupt those communities. We could arrest their leaders, raid their homes, break up their meetings and vilify them night after night on the evening news. Did we know we were lying about the drugs? Of course we did" (quoted in Blow 2017).

The war on drugs escalated during the 1980s under the Reagan White House. This escalation was sparked by the introduction of crack cocaine into urban areas populated by African Americans, where it quickly became a product that drug gangs fought over to maximize their sales to willing consumers.

Crack cocaine and powder cocaine are nearly identical pharmacologically; the major difference between them is how they are ingested and the swiftness and intensity of their effects (Gwynne 2013). White people had used powder cocaine long before crack appeared; in fact, powder cocaine back then was considered rather glamorous and trendy and overlooked by law enforcement officials. When crack appeared, however, it aroused great alarm. Law enforcement efforts across the nation focused on crack, and new legislation produced harsh legal penalties that imposed much longer prison terms for a given amount of crack than for the same amount of powder cocaine.

Although on the face of it these legal efforts and penalties were racially neutral, it was inevitable that they would target African Americans most of all, and so they did (Alexander 2012). The number of drug offenders in state and federal prisons greatly increased, and these offenders tended to be African American or Latino. The war on drugs, then, has in effect been a legal war against African Americans and, to some extent, Latinos. Law professor Michelle Alexander (2012:197) has noted that African Americans "are not significantly more likely to use or sell prohibited drugs than whites, but they are made criminals at drastically higher rates for precisely the same conduct."

Reflecting this circumstance, 31% of all state prisoners sentenced for drug offenses are African Americans (2015 data) (Carson 2018), even though, as noted earlier, only about 13% of the national population is African American. This alarming situation since the war against drugs began led a president of the American Society of Criminology, Alfred *president of the American society of criminology* ↓

Blumstein, to observe, "What is particularly troublesome ... is the degree to which the impact [of the war against drugs] has been so disproportionately imposed on nonwhites." Blumstein called the war on drugs "a major assault on the black community" and said that "if a similar assault was affecting the white community, there would be a strong and effective effort to change either the laws or the enforcement policy" (1993:4–5). Whether or not it was consciously intended, then, the legal war against drugs has been racially discriminatory and helps account for the racial disparities we see today in criminal justice involvement.

Q

] conclusion

RACE AND THE COLLATERAL CONSEQUENCES OF MASS INCARCERATION

As should be apparent from the preceding evidence, mass incarceration has fallen most heavily on the shoulders of people of color, particularly African Americans. For prisoners and their families generally, but especially for African American prisoners and families, mass incarceration has had a number of **collateral consequences**, or unintended by-products of mass incarceration that have caused significant social and economic harm. Criminologists consider these consequences an "invisible punishment" beyond incarceration itself that also disproportionately affects people of color: not just offenders, but also their families and communities (Muftić, Bouffard, and Armstrong 2016; Uggen and Stewart 2015; Wakefield and Wildeman 2014; Western and Wildeman 2009). We outline these consequences here to highlight their impact.

Q

Q2 mass incarceration affects on POC & fam

Consequences for Offenders

People convicted of felonies suffer the *pains of imprisonment*, to invoke a classic term by the sociologist Gresham M. Sykes (1958). By "pains" Sykes meant several types of deprivations and frustrations of living behind bars. These deprivations include fear for one's personal safety, the loss of freedom and autonomy, and the loss of heterosexual relations. Although Sykes wrote about the pains of imprisonment six decades ago, the problems he described have become ever worse with the rise of mass incarceration.

Despite a recent small decline in incarceration, U.S. prisons and jails remain severely overcrowded, and living conditions are substandard and even squalid, with abysmal health care and a high risk of violence from correctional staff and from other inmates (Ross 2016). Moreover, released inmates often face dim prospects for employment, educational opportunities, housing, and relationships with law-abiding citizens, all of which help people to refrain from committing crime (Uggen and Stewart 2015). All of these circumstances may help make many inmates a greater risk to society when they are released from prison or jail than before they went behind bars (Travis et al. 2014). As criminologist Todd Clear (2007:27) has observed, "Being in prison is a brutalizing experience, and people who are subjected to these experiences find it harder to adjust to free society again." Because mass incarceration has disproportionately affected African Americans, Latinos, and Native Americans, all of the collateral consequences for offenders have disproportionately affected these groups most of all. Relatedly, criminologist Bruce Western (2006) has observed that because incarceration creates significant employment problems for ex-inmates, mass incarceration has exacerbated the economic inequality of African Americans and other people of color.

In yet another problem, because convicted offenders lose the right to vote in most states, almost 6 million current and released prisoners are not permitted to vote. This number includes more than 2 million African Americans, amounting to about 8% of all voting-age African Americans. In Florida, Kentucky, and Virginia, at least one-fifth of voting-age African Americans cannot vote because they were convicted of a felony (Chung 2016). The disenfranchisement of so many African Americans probably affected the outcome of the 2000 presidential election, when the U.S. Supreme Court declared that George W. Bush won Florida and thus the national election, and at least seven U.S. Senate elections since the 1980s (Manza and Uggen 2008). Thus, even though most convicted felons lose the right to vote, this loss has affected African Americans most of all and reduced their electoral influence and political clout.

Consequences for Families

More than 2.7 million American children, equal to more than 3% of all children, now have a parent in prison or jail, and many more millions of children have had a parent behind bars at some time during their childhoods (Reilly 2013). Children suffer in many ways when a parent goes to jail or prison (Wakefield and Wildeman 2014). They suffer emotionally from the trauma of having a parent behind bars, and they suffer practically and emotionally from the loss of parental care and often the loss of income when a parent enters prison or jail. For these reasons, parental incarceration harms children's school performance and increases their likelihood of breaking the law during adolescence and even during adulthood (Muftić et al. 2016); it also leads them to have sleeping and eating problems (Jackson and Vaughn 2017). All of these consequences again disproportionately affect African American and Latino children (Western and Wildeman 2009): About 6% of African American children and 2% of Latino children have an incarcerated parent, compared to only 0.9% of white children (Christian 2009).

Consequences for Communities

Because of mass incarceration, close to 700,000 prisoners are released every year, almost all returning to their home communities. Many, and probably most, had few prospects of gainful employment before prison, and, as we noted earlier, they probably have even fewer prospects after prison. Many also entered prison with drug problems and mental health problems that were more likely to worsen rather than improve during their incarceration (Travis et al. 2014). When these many ex-prisoners return to their communities, they thus bring with them a host of problems, including possible criminal behavior, that their communities must endure. Thus, "mass incarceration makes disadvantaged neighborhoods worse," says criminologist Clear (2007).

Because mass incarceration disproportionately involves people of color, its impact on community well-being hits their communities especially hard. This harsh truth led the National Research Council report mentioned earlier to conclude, "People who live in poor and minority communities have always had substantially higher rates of incarceration than other groups. As a consequence, the effects of harsh penal policies in the past 40 years have fallen most heavily on blacks and Hispanics, especially the poorest" (Travis et al. 2014:. 5).

SUMMARY

1. The United States continues to face persistent racial prejudice, illegal racial discrimination, and racial inequality. African Americans, Latinos, and Native Americans are much poorer than non-Latino whites and are more likely to live in areas with substandard living conditions, to lack educational and employment opportunities, and to be victims of hate crimes and everyday racial slights.

2. Although African Americans comprise only about 13% of the U.S. population, they represent 33% of all prisoners. Latinos and Native Americans are also overrepresented in criminal justice involvement.

3. Debate persists regarding the degree to which this overrepresentation stems from more frequent criminal behavior versus the degree to which it stems from racial/ethnic bias within the criminal justice system.

4. To appreciate racial disparities in criminal justice involvement, it is important to keep in mind that very few people of color in fact commit conventional crime and that the corporate executives and other people who commit very harmful white-collar crime are almost always white.

5. Mass incarceration arose from the interplay of a complex set of factors, including a rising violent crime rate, changes in sentencing policy and procedures, and racial prejudice. The legal war on drugs also targeted people of color.

6. Mass incarceration has had negative collateral consequences for offenders, their families, and their communities. Because of racial disparities in criminal justice involvement, these consequences have fallen most heavily on African Americans, Latinos, and Native Americans.

KEY TERMS

collateral consequences. In regard to criminal justice, unintended by-products of mass incarceration that have caused significant social and economic harm

conventional crime. Violent crime, property crime, drug offenses, and other such "street crime"

correctional population. The number of people under correctional supervision: in prison or jail or on probation or parole

criminal justice involvement. Incurrence of one or more of the following official legal sanctions: (1) arrest, (2) conviction, and (3) sentencing, especially incarceration in prison or jail

ethnicity. A subgroup of the population with shared social, cultural, and historical experiences

felony. A crime for which the possible incarceration is at least one year.

mass incarceration. The U.S. policy since the 1970s of imposing longer and more certain prison terms for people convicted of conventional crime, resulting in quintuple the earlier incarceration rate

misdemeanor. A crime for which the possible incarceration is less than one year

race. A category of people who share certain inherited physical traits, including skin tone and facial features

racial discrimination. Harsher treatment and/or the denial of rights and opportunities because of someone's race or ethnicity

racial disparities. Outcomes that affect one race more than another race

racial prejudice. Negative attitudes and perceptions about social categories of people because of their perceived race or ethnicity

racial stereotypes. False or simplified generalizations about people because of their race or ethnicity

white-collar crime. Crime committed by individuals or organizations, including corporations and professionals, during the course of legitimate occupational activity

REFERENCES

Agnew, Robert. 2016. "Race and Youth Crime: Why Isn't the Relationship Stronger?" *Race and Justice* 6(3):195–221.

Alexander, Michelle. 2012. *The New Jim Crow: Mass Incarceration in the Age of Colorblindness.* New York: New Press.

Andersen, Margaret L. 2018. *Race in Society: The Enduring American Dilemma.* Lanham, MD: Rowman & Littlefield.

Beckett, Katherine, and Theodore Sasson. 2004. *The Politics of Injustice: Crime and Punishment in America.* Thousand Oaks, CA: Sage.

Begley, Sharon. 2008. "Race and DNA." *Newsweek* February 29. http://blog. newsweek.com/blogs/labnotes/archive/2008/02/29/race-and-dna.aspx

Bleyer, Jennifer. 2001. "Prison Converts." *Progressive* June:28–30.

Blow, Charles M. 2017. "The Other Inconvenient Truth." *New York Times* August 17. https://www.nytimes.com/2017/08/17/opinion/republicans-white-supremacy-charlottesville.html?_r=0

Blumstein, Alfred. 1993. "Making Rationality Relevant—The American Society of Criminology 1992 Presidential Address." *Criminology* 31(1):1–16.

Bonilla-Silva, Eduardo. 2018. *Racism Without Racists: Color-Blind Racism and the Persistence of Racial Inequality in the United States.* Lanham, MD: Rowman & Littlefield.

Bureau of Justice Statistics. 2018. All Data Analysis Tools. https://www.bjs.gov/index.cfm?ty=daa

Bureau, U.S. Census. 2017. "Quick Facts: United States." https://www.census.gov/quickfacts/fact/table/US/PST045216

Carson, E. Ann. 2018. *Prisoners in 2016.* Washington, DC: Bureau of Justice Statistics

Christian, Steve. 2009. *Children of Incarcerated Parents.* Denver: National Council of State Legislatures.

Chung, Jean. 2016. *Felony Disenfranchisement: A Primer.* Washington, DC: Sentencing Project.

Clear, Todd R. 2007. *Imprisoning Communities: How Mass Incarceration Makes Disadvantaged Neighborhoods Worse.* New York: Oxford University Press.

Crutchfield, Robert D., and Gregory A. Weeks. 2015. "The Effects of Mass Incarceration on Communities of Color." *Issues in Science and Technology* 32(1)(Fall). http://issues.org/32-1/the-effects-of-mass-incarceration-on-communities-of-color/

Du Bois, W. E. B. 1903. *The Souls of Black Folk: Essays and Sketches.* Chicago: A. C. McClurg.

Feagin, Joe R. 2014. *Racist America: Roots, Current Realities, and Future Reparations.* New York: Routledge.

Fortner, Michael Javen. 2015. *Black Silent Majority: The Rockefeller Drug Laws and the Politics of Punishment*. Cambridge, MA: Harvard University Press.

Gottschalk, Marie. 2006. *The Prison and the Gallows: The Politics of Mass Incarceration in America*. Cambridge: Cambridge University Press.

Gwynne, Kristen. 2013. "4 Biggest Myths about Crack." *Salon*, August 10. http://www.salon.com/2013/08/10/busting_the_crack_propaganda_myths_partner/

Hinton, Elizabeth. 2016. *From the War on Poverty to the War on Crime: The Making of Mass Incarceration in America*. Cambridge, MA: Harvard University Press.

Jackson, Dylan B., and Michael G. Vaughn. 2017. "Parental Incarceration and Child Sleep and Eating Behaviors." *Journal of Pediatrics* 185(June): 211–17.

Kaeble, Danielle, and Lauren Glaze. 2016. *Correctional Populations in the United States, 2015*. Washington, DC: Bureau of Justice Statistics, U.S. Department of Justice.

Kerner Commission. 1968. *Report of the National Advisory Commission on Civil Disorders*. New York: Bantam Books.

Kessler, Glenn. 2015. "The Stale Statistic That One in Three Black Males 'Born Today' Will End up in Jail." *Washington Post* June 16. https://www.washingtonpost.com/news/fact-checker/wp/2015/06/16/the-stale-statistic-that-one-in-three-black-males-has-a-chance-of-ending-up-in-jail/?utm_term=.c16e86d4031b

Kyckelhahn, Tracey. 2015. *Justice Expenditure And Employment Extracts, 2012—Preliminary*. Washington, DC: Bureau of Justice Statistics. http://www.bjs.gov/index.cfm?ty=pbdetail&iid=5239

Manza, Jeff, and Christopher Uggen. 2008. *Locked Out: Felon Disenfranchisement and American Democracy*. New York: Oxford University Press.

Minton, Todd D., and Zhen Zeng. 2016. *Jail Inmates in 2015*. Washington, DC: Bureau of Justice Statistics, U.S. Department of Justice.

Muftić, Lisa R., Leana A. Bouffard, and Gaylene S. Armstrong. 2016. "Impact of Maternal Incarceration on the Criminal Justice Involvement of Adult Offspring: A Research Note." *Journal of Research in Crime and Delinquency* 53(1):93–111.

Myrdal, Gunnar. 1944. *An American Dilemma: The Negro Problem and Modern Democracy*. New York: Harper & Brothers.

Nellis, Ashley. 2016. *The Color of Justice: Racial and Ethnic Disparity in State Prisons*. Washington, DC: Sentencing Project.

Pfaff, John. 2017. *Locked In: The True Causes of Mass Incarceration and How to Achieve Real Reform*. New York: Basic Books.

Piquero, Nicole Leeper, Alex R. Piquero, and Eric S. Stewart. 2015. "Sociological Viewpoint on the Race-Crime Relationship." In *The Nurture Versus Biosocial Debate in Criminology: On the Origins of Criminal Behavior and Criminality*, edited by Kevin M. Beaver, J. C. Barnes, and Brian B. Boutwell, 43–54. Thousand Oaks, CA: Sage.

President's Commission on Law Enforcement and Administration of Justice. 1967. *The Challenge of Crime in a Free Society*. Washington, DC: U.S. Government Printing Office.

Raphael, Steven. 2009. "Explaining the Rise in U.S. Incarceration Rates." *Criminology & Public Policy* 8:87–95.

Reilly, Katie. 2013. "Sesame Street Reaches Out to 2.7 Million American Children with an Incarcerated Parent." *Fact Tank*. Pew Research Center. http://www.pewresearch.org/fact-tank/2013/06/21/sesame-street-reaches-out-to-2-7-million-american-children-with-an-incarcerated-parent/

Reiman, Jeffrey, and Paul Leighton. 2017. *The Rich Get Richer and the Poor Get Prison: Ideology, Class, and Criminal Justice*. New York: Routledge.

Ross, Jeffrey Ian. 2016. *Key Issues in Corrections*. Bristol, England: Policy Press.

Shannon, Sarah K. S., Christopher Uggen, Jason Schnittker, Melissa Thompson, Sara Wakefield, and Michael Massoglia. 2017. "The Growth, Scope, and Spatial Distribution of People with Felony Records in the United States, 1948–2010." *Demography* 54(5):1795–818.

Smedley, Audrey, and Brian D. Smedley. 2012. *Race in North America: Evolution of a Worldview*. Boulder, CO: Westview Press.

Sykes, Gresham M. 1958. *The Society of Captives: A Study of a Maximum Security Prison*. Princeton, NJ: Princeton University Press.

Tonry, Michael. 2008. "Preface." *Crime and Justice: A Review of Research* 37:vii–viii.

Travis, Jeremy, Bruce Western, and Steve Redburn, eds. 2014. *The Growth of Incarceration in the United States: Exploring Causes and Consequences*. Washington, DC: National Academies Press.

Uggen, Christopher, and Robert Stewart. 2015. "Piling On: Collateral Consequences and Community Supervision." *Minnesota Law Review* 99:1871–1910.

Wakefield, Sara, and Christopher Wildeman. 2014. *Children of the Prison Boom: Mass Incarceration and the Future of American Inequality*. New York: Oxford University Press.

Wallis, Jim. 2017. *America's Original Sin: Racism, White Privilege, and the Bridge to a New America*. Grand Rapids, MI: Brazos Press.

Western, Bruce. 2006. *Punishment and Inequality in America*. New York: Russell Sage Foundation.

Western, Bruce, and Christopher Wildeman. 2009. "The Black Family and Mass Incarceration." *Annals of the American Academy of Political and Social Science* 621:221–42.

Zeng, Zhen. 2018. *Jail Inmates in 2016*. Washington, DC: Bureau of Justice Statistics, U.S. Department of Justice.

[2]

RACE AND PUBLIC OPINION ABOUT CRIME AND JUSTICE

Chapter Outline

Learning Questions

1. What is meant by implicit bias?
2. What are two examples of racial bias in news media coverage of crime?
3. Why is the link between racial prejudice and punitiveness troubling?
4. How does race/ethnicity affect fear of crime?
5. Why do African Americans and Latinos tend to have more negative views about the police than non-Latino whites do?

Some of the most interesting aspects of race, crime, and justice concern the news media and public opinion. Accordingly, this chapter discusses certain racial biases in news media coverage of crime and several racial differences in public opinion about crime and justice. We will see that public views about crime and justice often differ along racial and ethnic lines, owing to the different lives led by people of different racial and ethnic backgrounds and to their disparate criminal justice experiences.

RACIAL BIASES IN NEWS MEDIA COVERAGE OF CRIME

Racial and ethnic bias in news media coverage of crime is not new. Back in the 1870s, newspapers claimed that Chinese immigrants were kidnapping little white boys and girls, taking them to opium dens, and turning them into opium fiends. Three decades later, newspapers claimed that the use of cocaine, then a legal and popular drug, would give African Americans super strength and make them invulnerable to bullets! Three decades after that, newspapers claimed that the use of marijuana would make Mexican immigrants more violent. All of these ridiculous claims reflected deep-rooted racial prejudice back then against the Chinese, African Americans, and Mexican immigrants, respectively (Musto 2002).

Are the news media still biased today? We hear a lot these days about "fake news" and "alternative facts." Amid these charges, it is important for the news media to be as objective and accurate as possible. Most legitimate news media are indeed as objective and accurate as possible. Unfortunately, various biases do creep into their coverage regarding which topics and events are covered and what is reported when a topic or event is covered (Schiffer 2018).

One such bias is racial. This bias reflects the fact that many Americans harbor unconscious racial biases and stereotypes (Banaji and Greenwald 2016). Social scientists use the term **implicit bias** (also called *hidden bias*, *implicit prejudice*, or *hidden prejudice*) to refer to this unconscious racial bias (Russell-Brown 2017). Because implicit bias is so common, it also sometimes affects news media coverage. In particular, it affects what kinds of things get emphasized or neglected in coverage about newsworthy incidents and topics (Savali 2015).

Research Findings on Racial Bias in Crime Coverage

In the area of crime and justice, this implicit bias plays out in television and newspaper stories about conventional crime, especially violent crime. Research typically uses **content analysis** to document this bias. In this type of study, researchers watch a television news crime story or read a newspaper crime story and record information, if mentioned, about the suspect's race and the victim's race. They do this for a sample of crime stories in a particular city and then compare their results to police-generated crime statistics for that city.

If there is no media bias, then the percentages of African American and white suspects and victims in the news stories should resemble the percentages of those respective groups in the city's crime statistics. However, if researchers find that African Americans are overrepresented as suspects in crime stories, that finding indicates implicit media bias and suggests that news organizations somehow consider crimes committed by African Americans to be especially newsworthy. Similarly, if researchers find that whites are overrepresented as victims in crime, that finding again indicates implicit media bias and suggests that news organizations somehow consider white crime victims to be especially newsworthy.

So what does this body of research find? In general, it finds that news outlets are indeed more likely, when compared with actual crime statistics, to carry stories about homicides and other crimes when the following circumstances hold (Colleluori and Angster 2015; Dixon 2017; Ghandnoosh 2014; Surette 2015):

- when the suspect is African American or Latino rather than white;
- when the victim is white rather than African American; and
- when the suspect is African American and the victim is white rather than any other combination of suspect and victim racial backgrounds.

Beyond these findings, several additional types of media racial bias occur. First, newspaper crime stories about white victims tend to be longer than those about African American victims (Gruenewald,

Chermak, and Pizarro 2013; Washington and Wright 2015). Second, crime stories tend to portray African American and Latino suspects in a more menacing way than white suspects (e.g., handcuffed or in a mug shot) (Feld 2003; Wing 2014). Correspondingly, they tend to emphasize that white suspects are basically good people who just got into trouble because of family problems or other difficulties, while African American and Latino suspects were long-time offenders with drug problems. Third, they tend to portray white victims as rather virtuous and not responsible for their victimization, while portraying their African American and Latina/o counterparts as bringing trouble upon themselves because of drug use or other problematic behaviors (Slakoff and Brennan 2017; Wing 2014).

A final type of media racial bias involves general news coverage about people of color. Do news stories overall show people of color in a bad light or a good light? To investigate this question, researchers examine news stories featuring African Americans doing anything at all to see whether they are shown engaging in crime versus other activities. Findings indicate that these stories tend to feature African Americans as involved in crime rather than doing anything else (Heinz Endowments 2011).

Impact of Racially Biased Crime Coverage

The types of news media bias we have just seen have practical effects that are perhaps even more regrettable than the bias itself. Research suggests that biased coverage has at least three related effects: (1) it increases racial prejudice among whites; (2) it intensifies their perceptions of African Americans and Latinos as criminals; and (3) it increases whites' fear of crime and support for harsher punishment of criminals (Ghandnoosh 2014).

Reflecting these effects, whites greatly overestimate the proportion of crime committed by African Americans (Ghandnoosh 2014). One study had subjects watch crime news stories that did not show a suspect and gave no information about the suspect. Even so, almost two-thirds of the subjects thought they remembered seeing a suspect, and 70% of these subjects reported that the suspect was an African American (Gilliam and Iyengar 2000)! As one observer commented on this study, "When we think about crime, we 'see black,' even when it's not present at all" (quoted in Blow 2014:A19).

A recent report on media crime coverage concluded, "'If it bleeds, it leads,' goes the saying about local news coverage. But not all spilt blood gets equal attention. Researchers have shown that crime reporting... includes a tendency... to exaggerate rates of black offending and white victimization and to depict black suspects in a less favorable light than whites.... Given that the public widely relies on mass media as its source of knowledge about crime and crime policy, these disparities have important consequences" (Ghandnoosh 2014:22).

The next section examines racial differences in public opinion about crime and justice. If news media coverage of crime were less racially biased, perhaps some of the opinions of white people we will examine would be rather different.

RACIAL DIFFERENCES IN PUBLIC OPINION ABOUT CRIME AND JUSTICE

The United States is torn by race and ethnicity. Rather than being one big melting pot, Americans have disparate experiences in almost every phase of life based on their race and ethnicity. As the last chapter emphasized, people of color have higher rates of criminal justice involvement. But this involvement is not the only way in which their lives differ from those of non-Latino whites. They are also much more likely to live in poverty, to reside in substandard living conditions and in high-crime areas, to go to inferior schools, to receive inadequate health care, to experience employment and housing discrimination, and to face everyday racial slights (Andersen 2018).

The concept of *white privilege* nicely captures this fundamental fact of life in American society. **White privilege** refers to the advantages that non-Latino whites enjoy in their everyday lives, whether or not they are aware of these advantages, simply because they are white (McIntosh 2016). Examples of these advantages are:

- Whites can drive a car or walk down a street without having to worry that a police officer will stop them only because they are white.
- Whites can shop in a store without having to worry that a security guard will watch them simply because they are white.
- Whites do not have to worry about not being hired for a job, or promoted within a job, because they are white.
- Whites can assume they may live in any neighborhood they can afford without being discriminated against because of their race.
- Whites generally do not have to worry about being the target of racial slurs.
- Whites trying to hail a taxi or get a Lyft or Uber ride do not have to worry about being ignored because drivers fear they will be robbed.
- Whites in a hotel do not have to fear being mistaken for a bellhop, door attendant, housekeeper, or parking valet.
- Whites generally do not have to worry about becoming victims of hate crimes because of their race.

Many other examples exist, but the essential point is clear: People of different racial and ethnic backgrounds live very different lives, and people of color suffer everyday disadvantages that whites never worry about. Instead, whites simply do not have to think about being white as they go about their daily lives.

Because people of color and whites do live very different lives, they also have different opinions about various social, political, and economic issues (Pew Research Center 2016). These issues include matters of crime and justice, as we shall now see.

Race and Fear of Crime

One of the most studied views about crime and justice concerns people's fear of crime. A standard survey question to measure fear of crime is, "Is there anywhere right around here—that is, within a mile—where you would be afraid to walk alone at night?" Although this is not a perfect question (for example, it asks only about walking alone at night, not in any other circumstance, and it does not explicitly ask about being afraid of crime), most survey respondents appear to understand the question's intent.

Findings from the 2016 General Social Survey, a national sample of American adults, show that people's racial/ethnic backgrounds affect their fear of crime as measured by this question. As Figure 2.1 illustrates, African Americans and Latinos are both somewhat more likely than non-Latino whites to respond "yes" to when asked about their fear of walking alone at night. This racial/ethnic difference reflects where these three groups live: African Americans and Latinos are more likely than whites to live in large cities, which tend to have higher crime rates, and also within the high-crime areas of these cities.

Because women tend to be more afraid than men of walking alone at night, combining race/ethnicity with gender produces an illuminating comparison regarding fear of crime. Figure 2.2 shows this comparison. African American women and Latinas are most afraid to walk alone at night, while

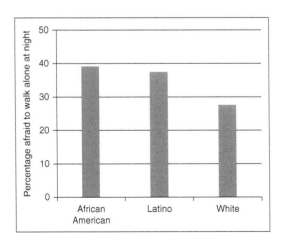

FIGURE 2.1 | Race, Ethnicity, and Fear of Crime

Source: Author's calculation from 2016 General Social Survey.

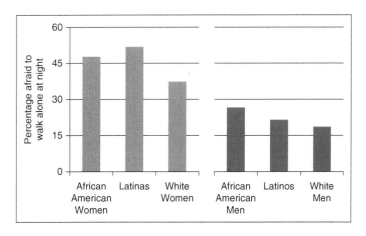

FIGURE 2.2 | Race/Ethnicity, Gender, and Fear of Crime

Source: Author's calculation from 2016 General Social Survey.

white men are least afraid. In fact, the former two groups are almost three times more likely than white men to report fear of walking alone at night.

Fear of crime has several negative consequences (Lane et al. 2014). It makes us afraid to go out at night or maybe even during the day, we worry about our children's safety when they go to school, and we worry about our own safety at home. It can also generate mistrust among people within high-crime neighborhoods and decrease small business activity if people do not want to be out and around. Given African Americans' and Latinos' higher fear of crime, all of these consequences affect them and their communities more than whites and their communities. In this regard, this difference echoes the differential impact we noted in Chapter 1 for the collateral consequences of mass incarceration.

Before we leave the subject of fear of crime, one more important finding should be noted. Research evidence shows that whites are more afraid of crime if they live nearer to higher proportions of African Americans, independent of the actual crime rates of the neighborhoods in which they live (Chon and Wilson 2016; Pickett et al. 2012). This effect reflects whites' stereotypical views regarding African Americans and crime as discussed in the preceding section on mass media racial bias.

Race, Racial Prejudice, and Punitiveness

A second view of crime and justice concerns **punitiveness**, or the belief that the criminal justice system should treat criminals more harshly. It makes sense to think that African Americans and Latinos should be less punitive than whites for two related reasons (Ghandnoosh 2014). First, because of racial disparities in criminal justice involvement (see Chapter 1), these two groups are more likely than whites to know or hear of someone of their own race who has been arrested, convicted, and/or sentenced. This awareness should prompt them to favor less harsh treatment of suspects and convicted offenders. Second, they should be more likely to favor less harsh treatment because they think the criminal justice system is often racially discriminatory. Much research finds that African Americans (and, when studied, Latinos) are indeed less punitive than non-Latino whites, or, to cite the reverse, whites are more punitive than African Americans and Latinos (Ghandnoosh 2014).

A popular measure of punitiveness involves questions about the death penalty. The 2016 General Social Survey asked a standard question of death penalty opinion: "Do you favor or oppose the death penalty for persons convicted of murder?" Although this is again not a perfect question (for example, it omits an alternative such as life imprisonment without parole), Figure 2.3 shows that African Americans are much more likely than whites to oppose the death penalty, while whites are much more likely to favor it. More specifically, about two-thirds of whites favor the death penalty, while only 40% of African Americans support it. Conversely, almost 60% of African Americans oppose it, compared to only about half that for whites. Latinos fall in between African Americans and whites in their death penalty views.

Racial Prejudice and Punitiveness

Research over the past three decades finds that whites are more punitive than African Americans or Latinos in part because they are racially prejudiced (Ghandnoosh 2014). In this way of thinking, many whites hold negative views and stereotypes of people of color, especially African Americans, including the belief that they are prone to violence and other

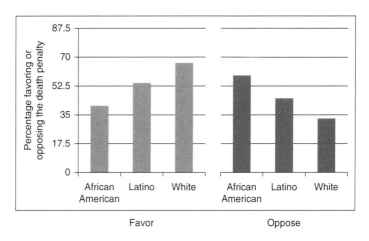

FIGURE 2.3 | Race/Ethnicity and Death Penalty Opinion
Source: Author's calculation from 2016 General Social Survey.

crime. This prejudice makes whites more likely to favor harsher sanctions by the criminal justice system to control people of color. If so, this effect helps explain why whites are more punitive than African Americans and Latinos, even though they are less likely than these two groups to be victimized by conventional crime (Ghandnoosh 2014). Supporting this argument, much survey evidence links whites' racial prejudice and stereotyping to greater punitiveness, including stronger support for the death penalty, after holding constant education, political views, and other relevant variables (Barkan and Cohn 1994; Brown, Socia, and Silver 2017; Chiricos, Welch, and Gertz 2004; Unnever and Cullen 2012).

An interesting survey experiment asked one group of whites simply whether they favored the death penalty, and asked another group of whites whether they favored the death penalty after first informing them that the death penalty "is unfair because most of the people who are executed are African Americans." Whites in the latter group were *more* likely than those in the former group to support the death penalty (Peffley and Hurwiz 2007). In another experiment, white subjects were shown videos that included photographs of California prison inmates. Based on random assignment, some subjects saw a video in which almost half of the inmates were African American, while other subjects saw a video in which only one-fourth of the inmates were African American. The first group of subjects was then less likely than the second group to sign a petition that would have made California's sentencing procedures less harsh (Hetey and Eberhardt 2014). When the white subjects perceived prison inmates as "more black," then, they in effect favored harsher sentencing.

The link between racial prejudice and support for the death penalty and other harsh treatment of criminals is troubling in a democracy that supposedly favors equal justice for all. To the extent that public opinion about crime and punishment influences criminal justice policymaking, the research evidence shows that this opinion "rests in part upon the racial prejudices of white Americans" (Barkan and Cohn 2005:312). Echoing this view, a recent report concluded that "white Americans' strong associations of crime with racial minorities have bolstered harsh and biased criminal justice policies" (Ghandnoosh 2014:3). Because racial prejudice should not be allowed to have this effect in a democracy, the research evidence on racial prejudice and punitiveness suggests that whites' views of crime and punishment should not overly influence policymakers.

Race and Views about Police

Police are the criminal justice professionals with whom the public has the most contact. This contact usually is for (alleged) driving offenses, but the police also stop and search people they deem suspicious, and they arrest those they think have committed a crime. Other people have contact with the police because they need help after a traffic accident, a crime incident, or other problems. Because the police play this large role in American society, much research studies the public's views about police and various aspects of policing.

Across all the questions asked, this body of research finds that African Americans and, less so, Latinos hold more negative attitudes than non-Latino whites about the police (Augustyn 2016; Fingerhut 2017; Weitzer 2014). In some examples from national surveys, only 18 percent of African Americans have confidence in the police, compared to 68% of whites (Bobo and Thompson 2006); 54% of African Americans say that the police "stop people on the streets of your city without good reason" very often or fairly often, compared to only 16% of whites (Weitzer and Tuch 2004); and 48% of African Americans say that police use excessive force against people in their city very often or fairly often, compared to only 13% of whites (Weitzer and Tuch 2004). When Latinos are included in these surveys, their views generally fall in between those of African Americans and non-Latino whites.

Scholars attribute these racial/ethnic differences in views of police to at least three factors. First, African Americans and Latinos have more contact with the police, and police contact of various kinds relates to more negative attitudes about the police (Augustyn 2016). Second, the contact that African Americans and Latinos have often involves negative experiences such as being arrested or being stopped and sometimes searched while driving or walking (Brunson 2007; Weitzer and Tuch 2006). Third, these two groups tend to live in higher-crime neighborhoods, where the police and residents often have an uneasy relationship filled with mutual distrust (Sharp and Johnson 2009). The negative views of police held by people of color is thought to hinder police efforts to control crime in their neighborhoods, in part because residents may be less willing to report crimes to the police or to otherwise cooperate with law enforcement when crimes are being investigated (Ghandnoosh 2014).

Related research investigates whether race affects public support for police use of force and other uses of police powers, and whether racial prejudice and stereotyping increase whites' support for these practices. This research finds that whites are indeed more likely to endorse these practices, and that racial prejudice and stereotyping increase their support for the practices (Barkan and Cohn 1998; Pickett 2016; Silver and Pickett 2015). This latter finding echoes our earlier discussion of the research on racial prejudice and punitiveness among whites.

To illustrate one such finding, Figure 2.4 depicts 2016 GSS responses to the question "Are there any situations you can imagine in which you

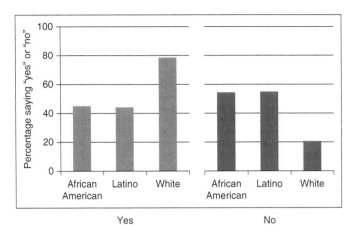

FIGURE 2.4 | Race/Ethnicity and Approval of Police Use of Force
Source: Author's calculation from 2016 General Social Survey.

would approve of a policeman striking an adult male citizen?" Whites are much more likely to respond "yes" to this question (left side of figure), while, conversely, African Americans and Latinos are much more likely to respond "no" (right side of figure).

Race and Perceptions of Criminal Justice System Injustice

Strong racial differences also exist for perceptions that the criminal justice system is biased or otherwise unjust: for example, that the death penalty discriminates against people of color, that the police do not treat everyone fairly, or that the local police commit brutality. Not surprisingly, African Americans and, less so, Latinos are more likely than non-Latino whites to believe that the criminal justice system is unjust in these ways (Gabbidon and Higgins 2009; Johnson 2008; Peffley and Hurwitz 2010; Unah and Wright 2015; Unnever and Gabbidon 2015).

To illustrate, 68% of African Americans in a 2013 national poll believed that the criminal justice system is biased against black people, compared to only 25% of whites. Similarly, a 2002 national survey found

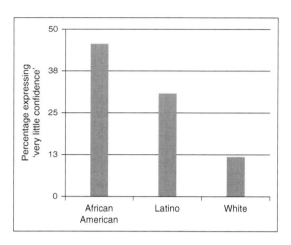

FIGURE 2.5 | Race/Ethnicity and Confidence in Police to Treat Blacks and Whites Equally, 2014

Source: Author's calculation using RoperExplorer (http://tinyurl.com/y8pjwyuc).

that about 75% of African Americans and 50% of Latinos felt that the local police treated minorities worse than whites, while 75% of whites thought the police treat everyone equally (Ghandnoosh 2014).

We can again depict the relationship between race and perceptions of injustice with national data. Figure 2.5 depicts the racial differences in the percentages of people who say they have "very little confidence" in the ability of their local police "to treat blacks and whites equally." African Americans are much more likely than whites to have very little confidence in this respect, with Latinos again in between these two groups.

Race and Explanations for Racial Disparities in Criminal Justice Involvement

In a final area of public opinion, some survey evidence examines why people think African Americans are disproportionately likely to be arrested and incarcerated (Peffley and Hurwitz 2010; Unnever 2008). This evidence finds that African Americans tend to cite a biased criminal justice system for this circumstance, while whites tend to cite young African Americans' disrespect for authority and actual higher rates of criminal behavior. In a related view, whites are more likely than African Americans to attribute criminal behavior to individual failings than to poverty, unemployment, and other structural reasons for crime (Thompson and Bobo 2011).

Summarizing Racial Differences in Public Opinion

U.S. racial/ethnic groups live very different lives. The evidence we have seen of racial differences in public opinion on crime and justice reflects this fact of American life. In particular, it reflects the fact that African Americans and Latinos are much more likely than whites to have negative experiences in the criminal justice system, and also that many whites are racially prejudiced and hold negative stereotypes of people of color. To cite the subtitle of an important book on this subject, African Americans and whites experience "separate realities" in their lives and criminal justice experiences and thus form different views about crime and justice in America (Peffley and Hurwitz 2010).

SUMMARY

1. News media crime coverage tends to be racially biased in several ways. Crime stories tend to overrepresent African Americans and Latinos as suspects and also to overrepresent whites as victims. They also tend to feature African Americans and Latino suspects in more menacing contexts than white suspects.

2. This biased coverage may increase racial prejudice among whites and intensify their perceptions of African Americans and Latinos as criminals. It may also increase whites' fear of crime and support for harsher punishment of criminals.

3. People of color and non-Latino whites live very different lives, as captured by the concept of white privilege. These different lives greatly affect their views on a wide range of social, political, and economic issues.

4. Compared to non-Latino whites, African Americans and Latinos are more likely to be afraid of crime, and less punitive regarding the punishment and other treatment of criminals. Research finds that white support for the death penalty and other punitive measures stems in part from their racial prejudice.

5. African Americans and Latinos have more negative views about the police, and they are also more likely to perceive that various aspects of the criminal justice system operate in an unjust manner.

6. African Americans are more likely than whites to blame racial disparities in criminal justice involvement on bias in the criminal justice system, whereas whites are more likely to attribute these disparities to individual failings and other failings in African American neighborhoods.

KEY TERMS

content analysis. Regarding the study of news media crime coverage, a research method in which researchers watch television crime stories or read newspaper crime stories and record such information as the suspect's and victim's race and the nature of the crime

implicit bias. Unconscious racial bias

punitiveness. The belief that the criminal justice system should treat criminals more harshly

white privilege. The advantages that non-Latino whites enjoy in their everyday lives, whether or not they are aware of these advantages, simply because they are white

REFERENCES

Andersen, Margaret L. 2018. *Race in Society: The Enduring American Dilemma.* Lanham, MD: Rowman & Littlefield.

Augustyn, Megan Bears. 2016. "Updating Perceptions of (In)Justice." *Journal of Research in Crime and Delinquency* 53(2):255–86.

Banaji, Mahzarin, and Anthony G. Greenwald. 2016. *Blindspot: Hidden Biases of Godo People.* New York: Bantam Books.

Barkan, Steven E., and Steven F. Cohn. 1994. "Racial Prejudice and Support for the Death Penalty by Whites." *Journal of Research in Crime and Delinquency* 31(2):202–9.

———.1998. "Racial Prejudice and Support by Whites for Police Use of Force: A Research Note." *Justice Quarterly* 15:743–53.

———. 2005. "Why Whites Favor Spending More Money to Fight Crime: The Role of Racial Prejudice." *Social Problems* 52:300–314.

Blow, Charles M. 2014. "Crime, Bias, and Statistics." *New York Times* September 8:A19.

Bobo, Lawrence D., and Victor Thompson. 2006. "Unfair by Design: The War on Drugs, Race, and the Legitimacy of the Criminal Justice System." *Social Research* 73(2):445–72.

Brown, Elizabeth K., Kelly M. Socia, and Jasmine R. Silver. 2017. "Conflicted Conservatives, Punitive Views, and Anti-Black Racial Bias 1974–2014." *Punishment & Society.* https://doi-org.prxy4.ursus.maine.edu/10.1177/1462474517736295

Brunson, Rod K. 2007. "'Police Don't Like Black People': African-American Young Men's Accumulated Police Experiences." *Criminology & Public Policy* 6:71–102.

Chiricos, Ted, Kelly Welch, and Marc Gertz. 2004. "Racial Typification of Crime and Support for Punitive Measures." *Criminology* 42:359–89.

Chon, Don Soo, and Mary Wilson. 2016. "Perceived Risk of Burglary and Fear of Crime: Individual- and Country-Level Mixed Modeling." *International Journal of Offender Therapy & Comparative Criminology* 60(3):308–25.

Colleluori, Salvatore, and Daniel Angster. 2015. "New York City Television Stations Continue Disproportionate Coverage of Black Crime." Media Matters for America. https://www.mediamatters.org/research/2015/03/23/report-new-york-city-television-stations-contin/202553

Dixon, Travis L. 2017. "Good Guys Are Still Always in White? Positive Change and Continued Misrepresentation of Race and Crime on Local Television News." *Communication Research* 44(6):775–92.

Feld, Barry C. 2003. "The Politics of Race and Juvenile Justice: The 'Due Process Revolution' and the Conservative Reaction." *Justice Quarterly* 20:765–800.

Fingerhut, Hannah. 2017. "Deep Racial, Partisan Divisions in Americans' Views of Police Officers." *Fact Tank.* Pew Research Center. http://www.pewresearch.org/fact-tank/2017/09/15/deep-racial-partisan-divisions-in-americans-views-of-police-officers/

Gabbidon, Shaun L., and George E. Higgins. 2009. "The Role of Race/Ethnicity and Race Relations on Public Opinion Related to the Treatment of Blacks by the Police." *Police Quarterly* 12(1):102–15.

Ghandnoosh, Nazgol. 2014. *Race and Punishment: Racial Perceptions of Crime and Support for Punitive Policies.* Washington, DC: Sentencing Project.

Gilliam, F. D., and S. Iyengar. 2000. "Prime Suspects: The Influence of Local Television News on the Viewing Public." *American Journal of Political Science* 44:560–73.

Gruenewald, Jeff, Steven M. Chermak, and Jesenia M. Pizarro. 2013. "Covering Victims in the News: What Makes Minority Homicides Newsworthy?" *Justice Quarterly* 30(5):755–83.

Heinz Endowments. 2011. "Portrayal and Perception: Two Audits of News Media Reporting on African American Men and Boys." http://www.heinz.org/ userfiles/library/aamb-mediareport.pdf

Hetey, Rebecca C., and Jennifer L. Eberhardt. 2014. "Racial Disparities in Incarceration Increase Acceptance of Punitive Policies." *Psychological Science* 25(10):1949–54.

Johnson, Devon. 2008. "Racial Prejudice, Perceived Injustice, and the Black-White Gap in Punitive Attitudes." *Journal of Criminal Justice* 36:198–206.

Lane, Jodi, Nicole E. Rader, Billy Henson, Bonnie S. Fisher, and David C. May. 2014. *Fear of Crime in the United States: Causes, Consequences, and Contradictions.* Durham, NC: Carolina Academic Press.

McIntosh, Peggy. 2016. "White Privilege: Unpacking the Invisible Landscape." In *Race, Class, and Gender: An Anthology,* edited by Margaret L. Andersen and Patricia Hill Collins, 74–78. Belmont, CA: Wadsworth.

Musto, David F., ed. 2002. *Drugs in America: A Documentary History.* New York: New York University Press.

Peffley, Mark, and Jon Hurwiz. 2007. "Persuasion and Resistance: Race and the Death Penalty in America." *American Journal of Political Science* 51(4):996–1012.

———. 2010. *Justice in America: The Separate Realities of Blacks and Whites.* New York: Cambridge University Press.

Pew Research Center. 2016. "On Views of Race and Inequality, Blacks and Whites Are World's Apart." http://assets.pewresearch.org/wp-content/uploads/sites/3/2016/06/ST_16.06.27_Race-Inequality-Final.pdf

Pickett, Justin. 2016. "On the Social Foundations for Crimmigration: Latino Threat and Support for Expanded Police Powers." *Journal of Quantitative Criminology* 32(1):103–32.

Pickett, Justin T., T. E. D. Chiricos, Kristin M. Golden, and Marc Gertz. 2012. "Reconsidering the Relationship Between Perceived Neighborhood Racial Composition and Whites' Perceptions of Victimization Risk: Do Racial Stereotypes Matter?" *Criminology* 50(1):145–86.

Russell-Brown, Katheryn. 2017. "Making Implicit Bias Explicit." In *Policing the Black Man: Arrest, Prosecution, and Imprisonment*, edited by Angela J. Davis, 135–60. New York: Pantheon Books.

Savali, Kirsten West. 2015. "Throw Away the Script: How Media Bias Is Killing Black America." *Root* June 2. https://www.theroot.com/throw-away-the-script-how-media-bias-is-killing-black-1790860024

Schiffer, Adam J. 2018. *Evaluating Media Bias*. Lanham, MD: Rowman & Littlefield.

Sharp, Elaine B., and Paul E. Johnson. 2009. "Accounting for Variation in Distrust of Local Police." *JQ: Justice Quarterly* 26(1):157–82.

Silver, Jasmine R., and Justin T. Pickett. 2015. "Toward a Better Understanding of Politicized Policing Attitudes: Conflicted Conservatism and Support for Police Use of Force." *Criminology* 53(4):650–76.

Slakoff, Danielle C., and Pauline K. Brennan. 2017. "The Differential Representation of Latina and Black Female Victims in Front-Page News Stories: A Qualitative Document Analysis." *Feminist Criminology*. https://doi.org/10.1177/1557085117747031

Surette, Ray. 2015. *Media, Crime, and Criminal Justice: Images, Realities, and Policies*. Belmont, CA: Wadsworth.

Thompson, Victor R., and Lawrence D. Bobo. 2011. "Thinking about Crime: Race and Lay Accounts of Lawbreaking Behavior." *Annals of the American Academy of Political and Social Science,* 634:16–38.

Unah, Isaac, and Valerie Wright. 2015. "Divided by Race: Differences in the Perception of Injustice." In *Deadly Injustice: Trayvon Martin, Race and the Criminal Justice System*, edited by Devon Johnson, Patricia Y. Warren, and Amy Farrell, 245–74. New York: New York University Press.

Unnever, James D. 2008. "Two Worlds Far Apart: Black-White Differences in Beliefs about Why African-American Men Are Disproportionately Imprisoned." *Criminology* 46(2):511–38.

Unnever, James D., and Francis T. Cullen. 2012. "White Perceptions of Whether African Americans and Hispanics are Prone to Violence and Support for the Death Penalty." *Journal of Research in Crime & Delinquency* 49(4):519–44.

Unnever, James D., and Shaun L. Gabbidon. 2015. "Do Blacks Speak with One Voice? Immigrants, Public Opinions, and Perceptions of Criminal Injustices." *Justice Quarterly* 32(4):680–704.

Washington, Heather M., and Valerie Wright. 2015. "Read between the Lines: What Determines Media Coverage of Youth Homcide?" In *Deadly Injustice: Trayvon Martin, Race, and the Criminal Justice System*, edited by Devon Johnson, Patricia Y. Warren, and Amy Farrell, 298–322. New York: New York University Press.

Weitzer, Ronald. 2014. "The Puzzling Neglect of Hispanic Americans in Research on Police–Citizen Relations." *Ethnic and Racial Studies* 37(11):1995–2013.

Weitzer, Ronald A., and Steven A. Tuch. 2004. "Race and Perceptions of Police Misconduct." *Social Problems* 51:305–25.

———. 2006. *Race and Policing in America: Conflict and Reform*. New York: Cambridge University Press.

Wing, Nick. 2014. "When The Media Treats White Suspects and Killers Better than Black Victims." *Huffington Post* August 14. http://www.huffingtonpost.com/2014/08/14/media-black-victims_n_5673291.html

[3]

RACE AND CRIMINAL BEHAVIOR

Chapter Outline

Learning Questions

1. What percentages of arrests for violent crime and property crime involve African American and Latino suspects?

2. Why do victimization and self-report data suggest that there are racial differences in conventional criminal behavior?
3. What is meant by a structural explanation of racial differences in offending?
4. Why are African American youths' crime rates lower than might be expected from their negative life circumstances?
5. What are the implications of white-collar crime for understanding racial differences in criminal behavior?

This chapter returns to a question raised in Chapter 1: To what extent do racial disparities in criminal justice involvement reflect differential involvement in criminal behavior by people of color (especially African Americans, but also Latinos and Native Americans), versus racial bias in the criminal justice system? To begin to answer this question, this chapter discusses the research evidence regarding differential involvement in criminal behavior. We shall see that the evidence does point to actual heavier involvement in serious conventional crime by people of color, notwithstanding possible racial bias in the criminal justice system. While acknowledging this truth, we will also emphasize the structural basis for this heavier involvement, in line with most criminologists who consider this issue.

EVIDENCE OF RACIAL DIFFERENCES IN CRIMINAL BEHAVIOR

The evidence scholars cite for racial differences in conventional crime comes from the nation's major sources of data on involvement in criminal behavior. One source is the **Uniform Crime Reports (UCR)** of the Federal Bureau of Investigation. The FBI gathers crime data from police precincts across the United States. The police provide data on crimes they learn about from victims and witnesses, including the age, race, and ethnicity of any person(s) arrested. The UCR is an imperfect source of crime data, partly because many victims do not report crimes to police (Mosher, Miethe, and Hart 2011). However, its arrest data do begin to provide a portrait of the kinds of people who are arrested for given crimes.

This portrait is incomplete for several reasons. First, most crimes do not end in an arrest (only about one-fifth of reported violent and property crimes end in arrest), so it is possible that the racial composition of the persons who are arrested differs from the racial composition of the offenders in the bulk of crimes with no arrests. Second, arrestees' racial composition may reflect police biases against one race and/or in favor of another race. Third, the offender's race may affect whether a victim or witness reports the crime to the police. Despite these issues, criminologists often use arrest data as a starting point for understanding crime trends and racial and other demographic differences in criminal behavior, and we will do the same here.

Race and Arrest

To explore racial differences in arrest, we will examine two types of comparisons. First, we will compare the percentages that U.S. racial/ethnic groups comprise of all arrestees with their percentages of the entire U.S. population. Second, we will compare the arrest rate per 100,000 population for these groups. These comparisons will consider UCR arrests for violent crimes and for property crimes. As measured by the FBI and UCR, **violent crimes** include homicide, aggravated assault, rape, and robbery, while **property crimes** include burglary, robbery, motor vehicle theft, and arson. These two categories make up what the FBI calls Part I offenses, while a host of other crimes, including public drunkenness, drug possession, prostitution, and vandalism, make up Part II offenses. In 2016, about 515,000 arrests occurred nationwide for violent crime, and almost 1.4 million arrests for property crime. Meanwhile, more than 6 million additional arrests occurred for Part II offenses. The total number of arrests nationwide in 2016 was about 8.4 million for all offenses (Federal Bureau of Investigation 2017).

Before we present the racial/ethnic arrest comparisons, two measurement issues should be noted that suggest caution in interpreting arrest rates for Latinos and whites. First, because not all police precincts report whether arrestees are Latino, arrest data for Latinos are less complete than arrest data for the racial categories. Second, most Latinos are white, and about 12% of all whites in the United States are Latino (Hixson, Hepler, and Kim 2011). The UCR's racial category of "white" thus includes a sizable number of Latinos. If, for the sake of argument, Latinos do have higher arrest rates than non-Latino whites, the UCR white category yields a somewhat higher arrest rate than if it included only non-Latino whites. To the extent this occurs, any racial difference in arrest rates involving whites will be at least somewhat smaller than if the white category included only non-Latino whites.

With these issues noted, Table 3.1 lists the percent distribution by race/ethnicity for violent crimes, for property crimes, and for all Part I and Part II offenses combined. African Americans represent a much higher percentage of all three categories of offenses than their 13% share of the entire U.S. population. This disparity is particularly true for violent crime, for which the African American share of arrests is almost three times higher than the African American share of the entire population. In data not shown in the table, this disparity is even stronger for homicide and robbery, for which the African American share of arrests is about 53% and 54%, respectively.

TABLE 3.1 PERCENT DISTRIBUTION OF ARRESTS BY RACE/
ETHNICITY, UNITED STATES, 2016

	African American	Asian	Latino	Native American	White
Violent Crime	37.5	1.4	23.8	1.8	59.0
Property Crime	28.1	1.2	16.4	1.7	68.7
All Offenses	26.9	1.2	18.4	2.0	69.6

Note: Because the UCR lists Latino/non-Latino arrests separately from racial category arrests, the percentages do not add up to 100% across the categories.

Source: Federal Bureau of Investigation 2017.

Because Latinos comprise about 18% of the population (see Chapter 1), they are somewhat overrepresented in Table 3.1 among violent crime arrests but not among the other two offense categories. Meanwhile, Native Americans' share of arrests in all three offense categories is about twice as high as their 0.9% share of the U.S. population. Finally, Asian Americans comprise about 5.6% of the U.S. population but less than 1.5% of all the offense categories.

It is again helpful to use rates to understand racial disparities in arrest. Doing a little math yields the following arrest rates per 100,000 population for all offenses combined (Federal Bureau of Investigation 2017; Semega, Fontenot, and Kollar 2017; U.S. Census Bureau 2016):

- African Americans: 5,393 arrests per 100,000
- Asians: 547 arrests per 100,000
- Latinos: 2,122 arrests per 100,000
- Native Americans: 4,268 arrests per 100,000
- Whites: 2,386 arrests per 100,000

Arrest rates are highest for African Americans and Native Americans and lowest for Asians.

Finally, let's examine arrest rates just for violent crimes:

- African Americans: 365 arrests per 100,000
- Asians: 30 arrests per 100,000
- Latinos: 137 arrests per 100,000
- Native Americans: 184 arrests per 100,000
- Whites: 98 arrests per 100,000

For violent crime, the African American arrest rate twice as high as the next highest rate, for Native Americans, and 3.7 times higher than the white arrest rate. The Latino arrest rate is somewhat higher than the white rate. Meanwhile, the Asian arrest rate for violent crime is again extremely low.

Chapter 1 emphasized that racial differences in crime rates primarily reflect the behavior of a small group of high-rate offenders rather than people more generally. To illustrate this important fact with arrest data, consider the African American rate for violent crimes of 365 arrests per

100,000 population of all ages. This rate is equivalent to just under 0.4%, which means that about 99.6% of African Americans were *not* arrested for violent crime in 2016. If we limit the population dimension of this rate to just adults 18 and older, the violent crime arrest rate for African Americans becomes about 487 arrests per 100,000 population 18 and older, or about 0.49%. This rate means that 99.51% of African Americans 18 and older were still *not* arrested for violent crime in 2016. As these numbers indicate, even if certain racial/ethnic groups in the United States do have higher crime rates, almost all people in the apparent "crime-prone" groups still do not commit crime.

Reliability of Race and Arrest Data

We noted earlier that arrest data are imperfect for understanding racial differences in criminal behavior. Although the arrest data we have just reviewed demonstrate racial disparities in arrest, the data do not tell us whether these disparities reflect real differences in criminal behavior or, instead, police bias, victim and witness reporting biases, and so forth.

These possibilities mean that we cannot automatically conclude from the arrest data that people of color are, in fact, more heavily involved in conventional crime. There is at least one crime for which arrest data are fairly reliable, or so criminologists think. That crime is homicide. Although only about one-fifth of all reported crimes are cleared by arrest, that figure rises to about 60% for homicide. Because homicide is such a serious crime, it is less likely that any police, victim, or witness biases will affect whether a known suspect is arrested for homicide. If homicide arrest data are thus fairly reliable, it is relevant to note that African Americans accounted for 53% of homicide arrests nationally in 2016, four times their 13% share of the U.S. population (Federal Bureau of Investigation 2017). Criminologists think this disparity does reflect African Americans' greater likelihood of committing homicide, despite the many homicides that do not end in arrest and possible police or witness biases (Hawkins et al. 2017; Piquero, Piquero, and Stewart 2015). Keep in mind once again that even if African Americans are more likely to commit homicide, only a miniscule percentage of African Americans commit the homicides that yield the racial disparity in the arrest data.

What about the other crimes? As noted earlier, criminologists use arrest data to begin to understand racial differences in crime. They then use at least two other sources of criminal behavior data to try to determine whether the race and arrest data are, in fact, reliable indicators of racial differences or, instead, indicators of police bias or other factors. These two sources are victimization data and self-report data, to which we now turn.

Victimization Data

Every year the federal government conducts the **National Crime Victimization Survey (NCVS)**. This survey involves tens of thousands of respondents ages 12 and older and asks them about violent and property crimes they have experienced within the past six months. The NCVS measures several crimes in which victims usually or always see their offenders: aggravated and simple assault, rape and sexual assault, and robbery. (Although homicide victims also see their offenders, the NCVS does not ask about homicide for the obvious reason that the homicide victims are dead.)

Respondents who report being a victim of one of these crimes are asked to report the race of the offender. These reports may be imperfect: It is not always easy to perceive someone's race even in the best of circumstances, skin tones may greatly differ even within a race, and race itself has no real existence according to anthropologists and sociologists (see Chapter 1). However, because the majority of violence victims know their offender, the NCVS considers their reports about the offender's race to be reliable (Morgan 2017). Overall, then, these reports do help assess racial differences in criminal behavior. Criminologists began using NCVS data for this type of assessment shortly after the NCVS was established in the early 1970s (Hindelang 1978).

In this regard, it is useful to examine the percentages of offenders whom NCVS victims perceive as African American, and also to compare these percentages with the UCR percentages of arrested offenders who are African American, even if various differences between the NCVS and UCR make this comparison inexact. Table 3.2 displays these two sets of percentages.

TABLE 3.2 COMPARISON OF NCVS AND UCR REPORTS OF
OFFENDER RACE, SINGLE OFFENDER VICTIMIZATIONS, 2010

(% AFRICAN AMERICAN)

	NCVS Offenders	UCR Arrests
Aggravated Assault	32.5	32.4
Simple Assault	27.5	30.2
Rape/Sexual Assault[a]	33.8	30.7
Robbery	53.8	51.5
All Violent Crimes	33.0	31.9

[a]NCVS data are for rape and sexual assault, while UCR data are for rape only.
Source: Beck and Blumstein 2017.

Two very interesting findings emerge from this table. First, the percentages of African American offenders according to NCVS victims are all higher than the 13% African American share of the national population. This difference is especially evident for robbery, as African Americans are four times more likely to commit robbery (at least according to NCVS victims) than their share of the national population. These NCVS data thus echo the indication from UCR arrests, discussed earlier, that African Americans are indeed disproportionately involved in serious conventional crime, as criminologists conclude from NCVS data (Bishop and Leiber 2012).

The second interesting finding from Table 3.2 concerns the very similar percentages of African American offenders in the NCVS and UCR. Assuming that NCVS data are fairly reliable indicators of actual racial differences in offending, this similarity suggests that arrest data may not be racially biased. If so, arrest data are also fairly reliable indicators of racial differences in criminal behavior (Beck and Blumstein 2017).

Self-Report Data

A third source of information on race and criminality is **self-report data**. Social scientists and government agencies have administered self-report surveys of delinquent and criminal behaviors to samples of American youths under age 18. These surveys' respondents are asked to report whether and how often they have committed illegal behaviors ranging from (depending on the survey) petty theft and drug use to aggravated assault and shooting at someone. They are also typically asked to report their age, gender, race, and ethnicity and to respond to questions about their relationships with their parents and friends and about other aspects of their personal backgrounds.

Self-report surveys are an invaluable source of information for many criminological topics. For our purposes, they provide important information on possible racial differences in delinquency. To assess these differences, scholars compare the percentages of youths from the various racial/ethnic groups who report having committed various acts of delinquency. This type of assessment has yielded four important findings (Bishop and Leiber 2012; Elliott and Ageton 1980; Farrington, Loeber, and Stouthamer-Loeber 2003; Hindelang, Hirschi, and Weis 1981).

First, African American and Latino youths are more likely than non-Latino white youths to commit serious violent and property crime. As was true for NCVS data, this finding suggests that racial differences in criminal behavior do indeed exist, despite possible biases in criminal justice processing.

Second, a small proportion, 5–6%, of all youths of color, commit most of the serious offenses committed by all youths of color. This finding reminds us that even if people of color commit crime at higher rates, most people of color do not commit crime.

Third, few or no racial differences exist in drug use and less serious offenses such as petty theft, shoplifting, and simple assault. Any racial differences in offending thus exist for serious crimes but not for minor crimes.

Fourth, the racial difference in serious offending in self-report data is smaller than the racial difference in arrest data for adolescents.

This finding suggests that youths of color are overrepresented in arrests and the juvenile and criminal justice systems more generally, even beyond their higher crime rates. This type of comparison suggests, but does not prove, that racial biases may be at work. Here it should be noted that African American youths may be more likely than white youths to underreport serious offenses in self-report surveys (Elliott and Ageton 1980). If so, the racial difference in offending may be greater than self-report data suggest and closer to what arrest data suggest.

Summarizing Racial Differences in Criminal Behavior

The data and other information presented in this section support the following conclusions, with which most criminologists would probably agree (Agnew 2016; Beck and Blumstein 2017; Bishop and Leiber 2012; Piquero et al. 2015):

- People of color commit serious conventional crime at higher rates than non-Latino whites.
- People of color commit minor conventional crime at about the same rates as non-Latino whites.
- The racial difference in serious conventional crime appears to exist despite any possible biases regarding who gets arrest, convicted, and incarcerated for conventional crime.

Putting all these conclusions together, it is fair to say that the differential involvement of people of color in the criminal justice system (see Chapter 1) reflects to at least some degree the differential involvement of people of color in serious conventional crime.

This general conclusion comes with several caveats. First, as we have been stressing, most people of color commit no crime at all. Second, a relatively small group of chronic offenders accounts for most or all of the racial differences in criminality. Third, even if racial differences in criminal behavior do exist, racial biases in criminal justice processing may still exist. Fourth, the apparent heavier involvement of people of color in serious conventional crime should not obscure the heavier involvement of white people in serious white-collar crime, a point mentioned in Chapter 1 and revisited in the last section of this chapter.

Race and Drug Offenses

African Americans accounted for almost 27% of all arrests for illegal drug offenses (possession or sale) in 2016, double their 13% share of the national population. Meanwhile, Latinos accounted for 20.3% of drug arrests, slightly higher than their 18% share of the population. However, evidence from various surveys finds that African Americans and Latinos are *not* more likely than non-Latino whites to use or sell illegal drugs (Spohn 2015). Although differential involvement in crime might exist for some offenses, then, it does not exist for drug offenses. As Chapter 1 noted and as Chapters 5 and 6 will reiterate, the legal war against drugs has fallen most heavily on African Americans and Latinos, even though their rate of drug offenses is no higher than whites' rate.

Immigrants and Immigration

Before we leave the issue of disproportionate involvement in criminal behavior, it is worth commenting on a related issue, whether immigrants to the United States commit more than their fair share of crime. When immigration to this nation increased a few decades ago, many politicians and members of the public feared these new immigrants were committing crime at an alarmingly high rate (Lamm 1981). Although immigration has actually decreased in recent years, this concern continues. In particular, President Donald Trump raised the ugly specter of violent crime by immigrants during his 2016 presidential campaign and has continued to do so since he became president in January 2017 (Bier 2017; Preston 2015).

Despite all this concern, much research finds no evidence that immigrants commit crime at a higher rate than nonimmigrants (Adelman et al. 2017; Landgrave and Nowrasteh 2017; Light and Ulmer 2016). This research instead finds that immigrants actually commit crime at *lower* rates than nonimmigrants, partly because of their strong social institutions: churches, families, and schools (Vélez 2006). Thus, immigrants commit much less crime than many politicians and members of the public continue to think. As a recent *Newsweek* headline put it, "Trump is wrong about undocumented immigrants and crime" (Bier 2017).

Leaving the issue of immigration, we have cited the best available evidence to indicate that racially disproportionate criminal involvement in serious conventional crime does appear to occur. We now turn to explanations for this involvement.

EXPLAINING RACIAL DIFFERENCES IN CRIMINAL BEHAVIOR

If racial differences in serious conventional crime do exist, why do they occur? Social policy considerations demand accurate explanations of these differences. For example, if we can understand the social factors producing higher crime rates by people of color, then our society can (hopefully) devise social policies that address these factors. We now turn to these explanations.

Rejecting Racist Explanations

First we must unequivocally reject racist explanations of racial differences in criminal behavior that were popular before a half-century ago and probably still exist today in the minds of some ignorant people. These explanations asserted that African Americans, Native Americans, and many immigrants were biologically inferior and even subhuman. As evidence of their alleged biological inferiority, these groups supposedly drank too much, committed too much crime, engaged in mob violence and prostitution, and were guilty of a host of other sins. This basic belief in the biological inferiority of people whose ancestry was not white and Anglo Saxon helped justify the enslavement of African Americans, inhumane treatment of Native Americans, and mob violence against immigrants (Brown 2009; Dinnerstein and Reimers 2009). It also formed the foundation of the eugenics movement a century ago, in which thousands of young women, disproportionately poor and African American, were sterilized against their will to prevent them from reproducing (Levine

2017). Reducing the crime rate was a reason given for this hideous practice (Rocque, Welsh, and Raine 2012).

No reasonable scholar today attributes racial differences in criminality to biological inferiority of people of color. If these differences do exist, they should not be taken as evidence of any race's biological inferiority or superiority. Instead, we must look to much more sensible explanations. Criminological explanations of racial differences in criminal behavior draw on more general explanations of this behavior. We now review these general explanations and discuss their relevance for the racial differences we have seen.

Crime and the Social Structure

Criminologists with a sociological orientation emphasize that crime is rooted in a society's **social structure**, or the way it is organized in terms of its economic and social inequality and the social and physical characteristics of the settings in which people live. A **structural explanation** of crime, then, emphasizes that people are more or less likely to commit crime based on where they stand on society's socioeconomic ladder and where they live. Those who live amid various negative life circumstances are more likely to commit crime than those who live more advantageously. Criminologists' recognition of this fundamental truth echoes the insight of W. E. B. Du Bois (1899 [1973]:242), an African American sociologist and one of the founders of American sociology, who said more than a century ago that crime "is a phenomenon that stands not alone, but rather as a symptom of countless wrong social conditions." Several structural explanations of crime emphasize these countless wrong social conditions.

Social Disorganization

One such explanation is **social disorganization theory**, which argues that crime will be higher in neighborhoods that have high rates of poverty, divorce, and residential mobility (people moving in and out of the neighborhood); weak community supervision of adolescents; and low levels of participation in voluntary organizations. In these neighborhoods, the strong social bonds and social control mechanisms that help prevent crime become weakened, resulting in higher crime rates (Friedson and Sharkey 2015; Walters 2016).

Poverty and Inequality

A related explanation focuses on extreme poverty (sometimes called *economic deprivation*) and **economic inequality**, or the degree to which people in an area differ in income. This line of investigation argues that poverty and inequality promote offending for at least two reasons (Bernard 1990; Pyrooz 2012). First, people living in extreme poverty experience anger, frustration, and economic need because of their circumstances. These reactions lead some of them to commit violent and property crime. Second, such people also experience **relative deprivation**, or the feeling that they are economically and otherwise deprived compared to other people in general or to people who live nearby. This feeling again fosters anger and frustration that in turn lead to criminal behavior.

Poverty and Children's Cognitive and Neurological Development

Recent scientific research reinforces the sociological emphasis on the role that poverty plays in criminal behavior. This research finds that several poverty-related problems impair infants' and children's cognitive and neurological development in ways that lead them to commit antisocial behavior throughout the life course. These problems include the following:

- **adverse childhood experiences (ACEs)**, such as hearing gunshots in the neighborhood, that produce chronic **toxic stress** (DeSocio 2015; Rocque, Welsh, and Raine 2015);
- maternal stress, which stimulates the fetal brain to become "biologically wired for stress reactivity, impulsivity, and prolonged activation of survival mechanisms" (DeSocio 2015:70);
- maternal use of alcohol, tobacco, and other drugs during pregnancy (David et al. 2014);

- inadequate maternal nutrition (Marques et al. 2015); and
- inadequate childhood nutrition (Jackson 2016).

Neighborhood Physical Characteristics

Another structural explanation for crime argues that some neighborhoods are more likely to become "deviant places" because of their **criminogenic** (crime-causing) physical characteristics (Pyrooz 2012; Stark 1987).

One such characteristic is *high residential density*: many dwelling units close together and many people living in close proximity. Where there is high residential density, people interact to a great degree, creating the chance for arguments and interpersonal violence; adolescents can easily find friends with whom to spend time, including getting into criminal trouble; and robbery victims and other targets of personal crime are present. Another criminogenic physical characteristic is the presence of *bars, taverns, and other alcohol outlets* (Pridemore and Grubesic 2013). These outlets' presence contributes to more crime because people drink and get into arguments and fights, and because the outlets' patrons are easy targets for robbery if they drink too much.

Implications for Racial Differences in Crime

All of these structural reasons help explain racial/ethnic differences in crime. People of color are much more likely to live in poverty, and they are much more likely to live in neighborhoods with the characteristics conducive to crime just outlined. Because people of color are thus "overly exposed to conditions that are conducive to criminal activity" (Piquero et al. 2015:46), they are more at risk for committing crime (Peterson 2012; Sampson and Wilson 1995). As criminologists Thomas L. McNulty and Paul Bellair (2003:5) assert, "African Americans and other minorities exhibit higher rates of violence than do whites because they are more likely to reside in community contexts with high levels of poverty, unemployment, family disruption, and residential instability. . . . If whites were embedded in similar structural contexts, they would exhibit comparable rates of violence."

Native Americans, Structural Disadvantage, and Crime

We saw earlier that Native Americans have relatively high arrest rates. If this means they have higher rates of crime, why do they? The scant research on Native Americans roots their crime in their serious structural disadvantage: Because Native Americans are so much more disadvantaged than non-Latino whites, their structural disadvantage very likely helps explain their higher rates of offending. For example, Noah Painter-Davis (2012) found that Native American homicide and robbery rates in California were greater in areas with higher rates among Native Americans of poverty, female-headed households, and unemployment, and with lower rates of educational attainment.

Families, Parenting, and Antisocial Behavior

Inadequate parenting is often to blame for children's antisocial behavior and later criminality (Farrington 2011). Children need to learn self-control and prosocial attitudes and behaviors from their parents, and some parents simply are not up to this task. Instead, their parenting style and practices encourage less self-control in their children and a greater tendency toward antisocial behavior.

At the risk of stereotyping, these parents tend to be low-income parents with lower levels of formal education (Bornstein and Bradley 2012). One reason for this is that these parents are more likely to live in neighborhoods filled with stress from crime, crowding, and noise. This stress may impair their parenting, as child development scholar Margaret C. Elliott and colleagues (2015:256) observe: "Stressful neighborhood conditions take a toll on parents' health and well-being and compromise effective parenting." Because parents of color are more likely to be low-income parents, their parenting practices may be less than ideal.

Scholars debate whether having only one parent puts a child at greater risk for antisocial behavior (Pardini, Waller, and Hawes 2015). In this regard, it is worth noting that low-income children are more likely to have only one parent. Assuming for the moment that having only one parent does promote children's antisocial behavior, low-income children are thus more at risk for this behavior. Because children of color are more likely to live in low-income households, they are also more at risk for antisocial behavior.

Racial Mistreatment, Perceptions of Injustice, and Criminal Behavior

People of color experience everyday discrimination and mistreatment. For example, they are more likely to encounter people who treat them disrespectfully and discourteously and who insult them (Lewis, Cogburn, and Williams 2015). Criminologists think this mistreatment increases the anger and frustration people of color already feel because of their life circumstances in a racially unequal society. People of color are also more likely to perceive that the criminal justice system is unjust and racially biased, and this belief may undermine their respect for law (Unnever and Gabbidon 2011). This combination of anger, frustration, and disrespect for law is yet another reason for their apparent higher levels of serious conventional crime (De Coster and Thompson 2017; Unnever and Gabbidon 2011).

Urban Life and the Code of the Street

A final explanation for racial differences in crime concerns the subculture of urban areas. Several decades ago, some criminologists attributed African Americans' higher crime rates to a "subculture of violence" that encouraged violent responses to insults and other perceived slights (Wolfgang and Ferracuti 1967). Other scholars called this view a stereotype and said that African Americans were no more likely than other Americans to approve of violent behaviors (Ball-Rokeach 1973; Erlanger 1974). The subculture of violence hypothesis faded because of this criticism, but a new version has become quite popular in criminological circles. This version argues that a **code of the street**, involving attitudes that encourage violence in response to signs of disrespect, characterizes poor, urban areas (Anderson 2000; Matsuda et al. 2013; Sampson and Wilson 1995). Because this view emphasizes that this street code arises from poverty and racial discrimination, it holds that these social problems are ultimately responsible for the higher crime rates of urban residents. To the extent this street code exists, it again helps explain racial differences in offending.

Summarizing Explanations for Racial Differences in Criminal Behavior

People of color do appear to commit serious conventional crime at higher rates than non-Latino whites. Much criminological theory and research attribute these higher crime rates to the poverty and disadvantaged communities in which people of color are more apt to live, and to the racial mistreatment they regularly experience. If white people lived in the same circumstances, their own conventional crime rates would be higher. This type of understanding suggests that policies that successfully address poverty and other problems of urban communities would greatly decrease racial differences in criminal behavior.

Postscript: Why Racial Differences in Criminal Behavior Are Not Stronger

Robert Agnew (2016), a former president of the American Society of Criminology, recently posed a provocative question: In view of the many negative life circumstances in which many people of color live, why are the racial differences in conventional crime not stronger? As we have noted, racial differences do not exist for minor conventional crime, and the racial differences that do exist for serious conventional crime arise from the actions of a small group of offenders rather than from people of color more generally. To Agnew, this situation means that racial differences in crime are in fact much smaller than might be expected from the negative conditions that many people of color experience. This puzzle led Agnew to try to explain in particular why African American youths do not commit more crime than might be expected from their life circumstances in a society filled with terrible racial inequality.

Agnew's explanation centers on four groups of *protective factors* in African American families and communities that help keep youths from committing crime despite the criminogenic conditions in which many live. These four groups, which Agnew calls the four "S"s, include (1) skills in coping; (2) strengths in the face of adversity; (3) social supports; and (4) social controls.

Skills in Coping

African Americans learn from an early age that they will be treated negatively because of racial discrimination. They thus attribute any mistreatment they experience to discrimination rather than to their own shortcomings. This response may help maintain their self-esteem and so reduce their chances of committing crime. African American children also learn from their parents and other people how to avoid the influence of any chronic gang offenders in their neighborhoods. These and other coping mechanisms help keep African American youths from becoming involved in crime.

Strengths in the Face of Adversity

Despite their life circumstances, African Americans generally do not have worse mental health than whites. This suggests that African Americans have developed the ability to endure despite their circumstances. Agnew argues that this strong sense of *endurance* helps African American youths resist criminogenic influences. Other strengths in the face of adversity, which are encouraged by family, friends, churches, and other parties, are African Americans' *positive racial identity* and *hope and perseverance in the face of oppression*. These traits also help to reduce criminal behavior tendencies.

Social Supports

African Americans have strong extended family ties, including with *fictive kin* (individuals who perform family roles for nonrelatives), and a high level of church involvement. These social supports help African American youth become resilient to the criminogenic influences of their neighborhoods and life circumstances (Burt, Lei, and Simons 2017).

Social Controls

Several social controls in African American communities help inhibit the criminality of youths. First, most African Americans have a strong moral code that is no different from that of other races, with African American parents very concerned about their children's behavior. Second, there is some evidence that African Americans have a higher sense than whites of social concern and empathy. Third, African American parents in high-crime neighborhoods tend to supervise their children very strictly to minimize their contact with high-rate offenders.

The Importance of Understanding These Protective Factors

According to Agnew, these protective factors have significant policy implications. If we can learn exactly which factors are most protective against criminal behavior, these factors "might be cultivated in at-risk youth" (2016:213). Understanding these factors also helps to correct stereotypes about African American families and lives and criminal behavior tendencies. As Agnew observes, "Rather than deviance and pathology, the more appropriate characterization for most African Americans is one of strength in the face of adversity" (p. 214).

WHITE-COLLAR CRIME: RACE AND CRIMINAL OFFENDING REVISITED

Chapter 1 noted that almost all white-collar criminals who come from the ranks of corporate executives and professionals are white, and thus that the issue of racial involvement in criminal behavior depends on what kind of criminal behavior is being considered. This reminder is worth repeating near the end of a chapter that has presented evidence of the differential involvement of people of color in serious conventional crime.

Serious conventional crime involves many millions of victims, some 14,000–16,000 deaths annually from homicides, and the loss of some $16–20 billion annually from property crime and robbery. These are worrisome numbers, and serious conventional crime remains a worrisome problem despite a dramatic crime drop in the United States since the early 1990s. As bad as conventional crime is, however, white-collar crime is far worse in terms of its financial and human toll.

Corporations routinely break the law by committing fraud and other complex financial crimes, marketing unsafe products, operating unsafe workplaces, and polluting the air, ground, and water (AFL-CIO 2016; Reiman and Leighton 2017; Tillman, Pontell, and Black 2018). These practices take money away from families and other parties, and they also kill people or harm them physically short of death. In just one recent example of such *corporate violence,* more than 200 people died over several years because General Motors and Toyota hid evidence of ignition switches that caused vehicles to suddenly lose power (General Motors) and of gas pedals that caused sudden acceleration (Toyota) (Harwell 2015; Hirsch 2014). A recent estimate put the financial toll of white-collar crime at almost $600 billion annually, a figure about 30 times greater than the financial cost of conventional crime listed just above, and the human toll at more than 97,000 deaths annually, a figure about six times higher than the number of deaths from conventional homicides listed earlier (Barkan 2018).

This digression into white-collar crime reminds us once again that the question of racial differences in criminal behavior depends on what type of crime we are discussing. Even if people of color disproportionately commit serious conventional crime, whites clearly hold the monopoly on far more harmful white-collar crime. When the public and politicians worry about crime and have in mind someone with a black or brown face (see Chapter 2), they too conveniently forget about white-collar crime and the people with white faces who almost always commit it.

SUMMARY

1. Arrest data provide evidence that people of color disproportionately commit violent and property crime.
2. Victimization and self-report data also suggest that African Americans disproportionally commit violent and property crime, but not to the extent suggested by arrest data.
3. Most criminologists attribute the higher serious conventional crime rates of people of color to the poverty and other negative conditions in which they live.

4. Everyday racial mistreatment and cultural codes that justify violent responses to perceived slights and insults are also thought to explain these crime rates.

5. African American youth crime rates are lower than might be expected from their life circumstances, and several sets of protective factors help explain why this is so.

6. Although people of color appear to commit serious conventional crime at higher rates, white people commit almost all of the white-collar crime that is much more damaging.

KEY TERMS

adverse childhood experiences (ACEs). Highly stressful events during childhood that may impair children's cognitive and neurological development

code of the street. A set of attitudes in poor, urban neighborhoods that encourages violence in response to signs of disrespect

criminogenic. Crime-causing

economic inequality. The degree to which people in an area differ in income

National Crime Victimization Survey (NCVS). An annual federal survey of tens of thousands of respondents who are asked about various crime victimizations they may have suffered

property crimes. As measured by the Federal Bureau of Investigation, burglary, robbery, motor vehicle theft, and arson

relative deprivation. The feeling of being economically and otherwise deprived compared to other people in general or to other people who live nearby

self-report data. In criminology, data from surveys that ask respondents to indicate whether and how often they have committed various offenses

social disorganization theory. The view that crime results from weakened social bonds and social control in neighborhoods with high rates of poverty, dilapidated housing, residential mobility, and other such problems

social structure. The way society is organized in terms of its economic and social inequality and the social and physical characteristics of the settings in which people live

structural explanation. The view that people are more or less likely to commit crime based on where they stand on society's socioeconomic ladder and where they live physically

toxic stress. Chronic, severe stress during childhood that stems from adverse childhood experiences

Uniform Crime Reports (UCR). The Federal Bureau of Investigation's system of gathering crime data from police precincts across the United States

violent crimes. As measured by the Federal Bureau of Investigation, homicide, aggravated assault, rape, and robbery

REFERENCES

Adelman, Robert, Lesley Williams Reid, Gail Markle, Saskia Weiss, and Charles Jaret. 2017. "Urban Crime Rates and the Changing Face of Immigration: Evidence across Four Decades." *Journal of Ethnicity in Criminal Justice* 15(1):52–77.

AFL-CIO. 2016. *Death on the Job: The Toll of Neglect.* Washington, DC: AFL-CIO.

Agnew, Robert. 2016. "Race and Youth Crime: Why Isn't the Relationship Stronger?" *Race and Justice* 6(3):195–221.

Anderson, Elijah. 2000. *Code of the Street: Decency, Violence, and the Moral Life of the Inner City.* New York: W. W. Norton.

Ball-Rokeach, Sandra. 1973. "Values and Violence: A Test of the Subculture of Violence Thesis." *American Sociological Review* 38:736–49.

Barkan, Steven E. 2018. *Criminology: A Sociological Understanding.* Upper Saddle River, NJ: Pearson.

Beck, Allen J., and Alfred Blumstein. 2017. "Racial Disproportionality in U.S. State Prisons: Accounting for the Effects of Racial and Ethnic Differences in Criminal Involvement, Arrests, Sentencing, and Time Served." *Journal of Quantitative Criminology.* DOI 10.1007/s10940-017-9357-6.

Bernard, Thomas J. 1990. "Angry Aggression among the 'Truly Disadvantaged.'" *Criminology* 28:73–96.

Bier, David. 2017. "Trump Is Wrong about Undocumented Immigrants and Crime." *Newsweek* May 1. http://www.newsweek.com/trump-wrong-about-undocumented-immigrants-and-crime-591629

Bishop, Donna M., and Michael J. Leiber. 2012. "Racial and Ethnic Differences in Delinquency and Justice System Responses." In *The Oxford Handbook of Juvenile Crime and Juvenile Justice*, edited by Barry C. Feld and Donna M. Bishop, 445–84. New York: Oxford University Press.

Bornstein, Marc H., and Robert H. Bradley, eds. 2012. *Socioeconomic Status, Parenting, and Child Development*. New York: Psychology Press.

Brown, Dee Alexander. 2009. *Bury My Heart at Wounded Knee: An Indian History of the American West*. New York: Sterling Innovation.

Burt, Callie H., Man Kit Lei, and Ronald L. Simons. 2017. "Racial Discrimination, Racial Socialization, and Crime: Understanding Mechanisms of Resilience." *Social Problems* 64(3):414–38.

David, Anna L., Andrew Holloway, Louise Thomasson, Argyro Syngelaki, Kypros Nicolaides, Roshni R. Patel, Brian Sommerlad, Amie Wilson, William Martin, and Lyn S. Chitty. 2014. "A Case-Control Study of Maternal Periconceptual and Pregnancy Recreational Drug Use and Fetal Malformation Using Hair Analysis." *PLOS One* 9(10):1–10.

De Coster, Stacy, and Maxine S. Thompson. 2017. "Race and General Strain Theory: Microaggressions as Mundane Extreme Environmental Stresses." *JQ: Justice Quarterly* 34(5):903–30.

DeSocio, Janiece. 2015. "A Call to Action: Reducing Toxic Stress during Pregnancy and Early Childhood." *Journal of Child & Adolescent Psychiatric Nursing* 28(2):70–71.

Dinnerstein, Leonard, and David M. Reimers. 2009. *Ethnic Americans: A History of Immigration*. New York: Columbia University Press.

Du Bois, W. E. B. 1899 [1973]. *The Philadelphia Negro: A Social Study*. Philadelphia: Publications of the University of Pennsylvania.

Elliott, Delbert S., and Suzanne S. Ageton. 1980. "Reconciling Race and Class Differences in Self-Reported and Official Estimates of Delinquency." *American Sociological Review* 45:95–100.

Elliott, Margaret C., Veronique Dupéré, and Tama Leventhal. 2015. "Neighborhood Context and the Development of Criminal and Antisocial Behavior." In *The Development of Criminal and Antisocial Behavior: Theory, Research and Practical Applications*, edited by Julien Morizot and Lila Kazemian, 253–65. New York: Springer.

Erlanger, Howard S. 1974. "The Empirical Status of the Subculture of Violence Thesis." *Social Problems* 22:280–92.

Farrington, David P. 2011. "Families and Crime." In *Crime and Public Policy*, edited by James Q. Wilson and Joan Petersilia, 130–57. New York: Oxford University Press.

Farrington, David P., Rolf Loeber, and Magda Stouthamer-Loeber. 2003. "How Can the Relationship between Race and Violence Be Explained?" In *Violent*

Crime: Assessing Race and Ethnic Differences, edited by Darnell F. Hawkins, 213–37. Cambridge: Cambridge University Press.

Federal Bureau of Investigation. 2017. *Crime in the United States, 2016.* Washington, DC: Federal Bureau of Investigation.

Friedson, Michael, and Patrick Sharkey. 2015. "Violence and Neighborhood Disadvantage after the Crime Decline." *Annals of the American Academy of Political & Social Science* 660(1):341–58.

Harwell, Drew. 2015. "Why General Motors' $900 Million Fine for a Deadly Defect Is Just a Slap on the Wrist." *Washington Post* September 17. https://www.washingtonpost.com/news/business/wp/2015/09/17/why-general-motors-900-million-fine-for-a-deadly-defect-is-just-a-slap-on-the-wrist/

Hawkins, Darnell F., Jerome B. McKean, Norman A. White, and Christine Martin. 2017. *Roots of African American Violence: Ethnocentrism, Cultural Diversity, and Racism.* Boulder, CO: Lynne Rienner.

Hindelang, Michael J. 1978. "Race and Involvement in Common Law Personal Crimes." *American Sociological Review* 43:93–109.

Hindelang, Michael J., Travis Hirschi, and Joseph G. Weis. 1981. *Measuring Delinquency.* Beverly Hills: Sage.

Hirsch, Jerry. 2014. "Toyota Admits Deceiving Consumers; $1.2-Billion Is Record." *Los Angeles Times* March 19. http://articles.latimes.com/2014/mar/19/business/la-fi-toyota-settlement-20140320

Hixson, Lindsay, Bradford B. Hepler, and Myoung Ouk Kim. 2011. *The White Population: 2010.* Washington, DC: U.S. Census Bureau.

Jackson, Dylan B. 2016. "The Link between Poor Quality Nutrition and Childhood Antisocial Behavior: A Genetically Informative Analysis." *Journal of Criminal Justice* 44:13–20.

Lamm, Richard D. 1981. "America Needs Fewer Immigrants." *New York Times* July 12. http://www.nytimes.com/1981/07/12/opinion/america-needs-fewer-immigrants.html

Landgrave, Michelangelo, and Alex Nowrasteh. 2017. *Criminal Immigrants: Their Numbers, Demographics, and Countries of Origin.* Washington, DC: Cato Institute.

Levine, Philippa. 2017. *Eugenics: A Very Short Introduction.* New York: Oxford University Press.

Lewis, Tené T., Courtney D. Cogburn, and David R. Williams. 2015. "Self-Reported Experiences of Discrimination and Health: Scientific Advances, Ongoing Controversies, and Emerging Issues." *Annual Review of Clinical Psychology* 11:407–40.

Light, Michael T., and Jeffery T. Ulmer. 2016. "Explaining the Gaps in White, Black, and Hispanic Violence since 1990: Accounting for Immigration, Incarceration, and Inequality." *American Sociological Review* 81:290–315.

Marques, Andrea Horvath, Anne-Lise Bjørke-Monsen, Antônio L. Teixeira, and Marni N. Silverman. 2015. "Maternal Stress, Nutrition and Physical Activity: Impact on Immune Function, CNS Development and Psychopathology." *Brain Research* 1617:28–46.

Matsuda, Kristy N., Chris Melde, Terrance J. Taylor, Adrienne Freng, and Finn-Aage Esbensen. 2013. "Gang Membership and Adherence to the 'Code of the Street.'" *Justice Quarterly* 30:440–68.

McNulty, Thomas L., and Paul E. Bellair. 2003. "Explaining Racial and Ethnic Differences in Adolescent Violence: Structural Disadvantage, Family Well-Being, and Social Capital." *Justice Quarterly* 20:1–31.

Morgan, Rachel E. 2017. *Race and Hispanic Origin of Victims and Offenders, 2012–15.* Washington, DC: Bureau of Justice Statistics, U.S. Department of Justice.

Mosher, Clayton J., Terance D. Miethe, and Timothy C. Hart. 2011. *The Mismeasure of Crime.* Thousand Oaks, CA: Sage.

Painter-Davis, Noah. 2012. "Structural Disadvantage and American Indian Homicide and Robbery Offending." *Homicide Studies* 16(3):219–37.

Pardini, Dustin A., Rebecca Waller, and Samuel W. Hawes. 2015. "Familial Influences on the Development of Serious Conduct Problems and Delinquency." Iin *The Development of Criminal and Antisocial Behavior: Theory, Research and Practical Applications,* edited by Julien Morizot and Lila Kazemian, 201–20. New York: Springer.

Peterson, Ruth D. 2012. "The Central Place of Race in Crime and Justice: The American Society of Criminology's 2011 Sutherland Address." *Criminology* 50(2):303–28.

Piquero, Nicole Leeper, Alex R. Piquero, and Eric S. Stewart. 2015. "Sociological Viewpoint on the Race-Crime Relationship." In *The Nurture versus Biosocial Debate in Criminology: On the Origins of Criminal Behavior and Criminality,* edited by Kevin M. Beaver, J. C. Barnes, and Brian B. Boutwell, 43–54. Thousand Oaks, CA: Sage.

Preston, Julia. 2015. "Trump's Immigration Plan Returns to Familiar Strategy." *New York Times* August 18:A17.

Pridemore, William Alex, and Tony H. Grubesic. 2013. "Alcohol Outlets and Community Levels of Interpersonal Violence: Spatial Density, Outlet Type, and Seriousness of Assault." *Journal of Research in Crime & Delinquency* 50(1):132–59.

Pyrooz, David C. 2012. "Structural Covariates of Gang Homicide in Large U.S. Cities." *Journal of Research in Crime & Delinquency* 49(4):489–518.

Reiman, Jeffrey, and Paul Leighton. 2017. *The Rich Get Richer and the Poor Get Prison: Ideology, Class, and Criminal Justice.* New York: Routledge.

Rocque, Michael, Brandon C. Welsh, and Adrian Raine. 2012. "Biosocial Criminology and Modern Crime Prevention." *Journal of Criminal Justice* 40(4):306–12.

———. 2015. "Policy Implications of Biosocial Criminology: Crime Prevention and Offender Rehabilitation." In *The Nurture versus Biosocial Debate in Criminology,* edited by Kevin M. Beaver, J. C. Barnes, and Brian B. Boutwell, 431–35. Thousand Oaks, CA: Sage.

Sampson, Robert J., and William Julius Wilson. 1995. "Toward a Theory of Race, Crime, and Urban Inequality." In *Crime and Inequality,* edited by John Hagan and Ruth D. Peterson, 37–54. Stanford, CA: Stanford University Press.

Semega, Jessica L., Kayla R. Fontenot, and Melissa A. Kollar. 2017. *Income and Poverty in the United States: 2016.* Washington, DC: U.S. Census Bureau.

Spohn, Cassia. 2015. "Race, Crime, and Punishment in the Twentieth and Twenty-First Centuries." *Crime and Justice* 44(1):49–97.

Stark, Rodney. 1987. "Deviant Places: A Theory of the Ecology of Crime." *Criminology* 25:893–911.

Tillman, Robert H., Henry N. Pontell, and William K. Black. 2018. *Financial Crime and Crises in the Era of False Profits.* New York: Oxford University Press.

U.S. Census Bureau. 2016. "Facts for Features: American Indian and Alaska Native Heritage Month: November 2016." https://www.census.gov/newsroom/facts-for-features/2016/cb16-ff22.html

Unnever, James D., and Shaun L. Gabbidon. 2011. *A Theory of African American Offending: Race, Racism, and Crime.* New York: Routledge.

Vélez, María B. 2006. "Toward an Understanding of the Lower Rates of Homicide in Latino versus Black Neighborhoods: A Look at Chicago." In *The Many Colors of Crime: Inequalities of Race, Ethnicity, and Crime in America,* edited by Ruth D. Peterson, Lauren J. Krivo, and John Hagan, 91–107. New York: New York University Press.

Walters, Glenn D. 2016. "Neighborhood Context, Youthful Offending, and Peer Selection." *Criminal Justice Review* 41(1):5–20.

Wolfgang, Marvin E., and Franco Ferracuti. 1967. *The Subculture of Violence.* London: Social Science Paperbacks.

[4]

RACE AND CRIMINAL VICTIMIZATION

Chapter Outline

Racial Differences in Criminal Victimization
    Homicide
    Nonfatal Violent Crime and Property Crime
    The Intraracial Nature of Criminal Victimization
Explaining Racial Differences in Criminal Victimization
    Structural Factors and Criminal Victimization
    Individual Factors and Criminal Victimization
    Summarizing Reasons for Racial Differences in Criminal
        Victimization
Why Racial Differences in Criminal Victimization Are Significant

Learning Questions

1. For which specific crime is the difference between African American and white victimization rates especially pronounced?
2. Which race most victimizes non-Latino whites?
3. What are any two structural factors that explain racial differences in criminal victimization?
4. What does lifestyle theory say?
5. Why are racial differences in criminal victimization significant?

Three related observations from Chapter 2 provide the context for this current chapter: (1) News media crime coverage tends to overrepresent African Americans and Latinos as criminals and white people as victims, (2) white people tend to think it will be African Americans and Latinos who might victimize them, and (3) whites' racial prejudice against African Americans and Latinos fuels their support for harsher criminal punishment, stronger police powers, and other "tough on crime" measures.

Against this backdrop, the **criminal victimization** of African Americans and other people of color can too easily go unnoticed. Meanwhile, whites' fears that African Americans and Latinos will attack or rob them help underlie their punitiveness, which then may impel lawmakers to enact legislation yielding harsher punishment. These circumstances make it important to understand the racial context of criminal victimization in order to help dispel false beliefs concerning it. This understanding would also help direct funding and programming to the populations and communities with the highest rates of victimization.

In the service of these goals, this chapter discusses the racial dimensions of criminal victimization. As will become clear, racial differences in criminal victimization do exist, with people of color more likely to be victimized by violence, and with their higher rates of victimization reflecting their negative life circumstances.

RACIAL DIFFERENCES IN CRIMINAL VICTIMIZATION

To examine racial differences in victimization, we begin with homicide and then consider other types of violence as well as property crime.

Homicide

The largest racial difference in victimization occurs for homicide. Although African Americans comprise only about 13% of the national population, they account for about 52% of homicide victims (Federal Bureau of Investigation 2017). The difference is smaller for Latinos, who comprise about 18% of the national population but account for about 20%

of homicide victims for which victims' ethnicity was known. We can compare the homicide victimization rates of African Americans, Latinos, and whites by examining their number of homicide victims per 100,000 persons of each race. Figure 4.1 presents these rates and shows a striking difference: African Americans are about seven times more likely than whites to become homicide victims. Although homicide is still an extremely rare event, this difference is still troubling. Meanwhile, the Latino homicide victimization rate is slightly higher than the white rate.

Nonfatal Violent Crime and Property Crime

Racial differences in victimization for other types of crimes are much smaller but still apparently exist. We will use data from the National Crime Victimization Survey (NCVS) to present these differences. As a reminder, the NCVS excludes homicide because its methodology involves interviewing victims of crime (see Chapter 3). As you see in Table 4.1, African Americans have the highest victimization rate for all nonfatal violent crime and for serious violent crime, while Latinos have the highest victimization rate for all property crime. The rates for Latinos and

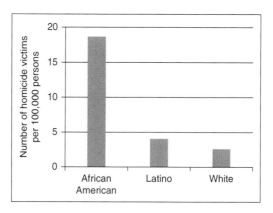

FIGURE 4.1 | Race and Homicide Victimization (homicide victims per 100,000 persons), 2016

Source: Federal Bureau of Investigation 2017; Semega, Fontenot, and Kollar 2017.

TABLE 4.1 RACE, ETHNICITY, AND CRIMINAL VICTIMIZATION,
NCVS, 2012–2015

(average annual victimizations per 1,000 persons ages 12 or older for violent
crime or per 1,000 households for property crime)

	All Violent Crime	Serious Violent Crime	Property Crime
African American	26.1	9.8	138.9
Latino	20.6	8.1	162.5
White (non-Latino)	21.3	6.7	120.0

Notes: Violent crime includes aggravated assault, simple assault, rape and sexual assault, and robbery; serious violent crime includes aggravated assault, rape and sexual assault, and robbery; property crime includes household burglary, motor vehicle theft, and personal theft.

Source: Bureau of Justice Statistics 2017.

non-Latino whites are rather similar for victimization by all violent crime, while Latinos have a higher victimization rate for serious violent crime.

Although these various differences are generally not statistically significant within any one of the four years on which Table 4.1's annual averages are based, the four-year averages do suggest some racial/ethnic differences in victimization. Doing a little math, the African American rate for all violent crime victimization is 23% higher than the white rate; the African American rate for serious violent crime victimization is 46% higher than the white rate; and the Latino rate for serious violent crime victimization is 21% higher than the white rate.

Beyond the national NCVS data just examined, criminologists also consider data for specific cities. In this regard, racial/ethnic differences in victimization are higher in some cities than for the nation as a whole. For example, a recent study of Chicago adolescents found that African American and Latino teens were twice as likely as white teens to be victimized by violent crime, a ratio that exceeds the national differences reported in Table 4.1 (Madero-Hernandez and Fisher 2016). This city evidence combines with the national evidence to yield the following conclusion: "For the three largest racial and ethnic groups in the United States—Blacks, Whites, and Hispanics—a consistent finding is that Blacks and Hispanics are the most violently victimized groups" (Madero-Hernandez and Fisher 2016:2).

Native American Victimization

Data on the criminal victimization of Native Americans are scarce, and the NCVS issues reports on their victimization only rarely. The most recent such report covered Native American victimization for the 1992–2002 period (Perry 2004). The central conclusion of this report was as follows: "The findings reveal a disturbing picture of the victimization of American Indians and Alaska Natives. The rate of violent crime estimated from self-reported victimizations for American Indians is well above that of other U.S. racial or ethnic groups and is more than twice the national average" (Perry 2004:iii).

Victimization rates for the report's decade-long period support this harsh conclusion. Native Americans experienced an annual average of 101 violent victimizations per 1,000 persons 12 and older, compared to 50 for African Americans, 41 for whites, and 22 for Asians. The Native American victimization rate was thus twice as high as the African American rate. Recent national evidence finds that Native Americans' victimization rates for sexual violence and for intimate-partner physical violence are also higher than those for non-Latino whites (Rosay 2016).

The Intraracial Nature of Criminal Victimization

Before turning to explanations for racial/ethnic differences in victimization, it is important to examine the racial backgrounds of offenders and victims. As the beginning of this chapter recalled, news media coverage implies that people of color, and especially African Americans, prey on white victims, and whites tend to especially fear this type of crime. In reality, however, most crime is **intraracial**, meaning that it occurs within a race: African Americans tend to be victimized by other African Americans, whites tend to be victimized by other whites, and Latinos tend to be victimized by other Latinos. This pattern reflects the idea that violent crime arises out of interaction with other people (Felson and Eckert 2016). We tend to interact most with people of our own race/ethnicity and thus are more apt to be victimized by them than by people from a different race/ethnicity (Kim et al. 2016). In general, homicide is the most intraracial serious crime and robbery is the least intraracial crime, with assault (aggravated and simple) and rape and sexual assault falling in between (Kim et al. 2016).

To illustrate the intraracial nature of homicide, Table 4.2 presents the percentages of homicide victims killed by members of their own race/ethnicity versus another race/ethnicity. Contrary to what whites might fear, four of every five white homicide victims (82%) are killed by other whites, and only 15% are killed by African Americans. Although white homicides are somewhat more **interracial** (occurring between races) than African American homicides, whites are still 5.5 times more likely to be murdered by other whites than by African Americans. Meanwhile, most African American homicide victims, 90%, are killed by other African Americans, while two-thirds of Latino homicide victims are killed by other Latinos.

To illustrate the intraracial nature of nonfatal violence, Table 4.3 presents the appropriate percentages from NCVS data. Almost 69% of white victims are victimized by other whites, while only 18% are victimized by African

TABLE **4.2** RACE AND ETHNICITY OF HOMICIDE VICTIMS AND
OFFENDERS, 2016 (%)

	Race/Ethnicity of Victim		
Race/Ethnicity of Offender	*African American*	*Latino*	*White*
African American	90	—	15
Latino	—	67	—
White	8	—	82

Notes: Data are for single offender/single victim homicides; African American and white categories include Latinos of those races.

Source: Author's calculation from data in Federal Bureau of Investigation 2017.

TABLE 4.3 RACE AND ETHNICITY OF NONFATAL VIOLENCE VICTIMS
AND OFFENDERS, 2012–2015 (%)

	Race/Ethnicity of Victim		
Race/Ethnicity of Offender	*African American*	*Latino*	*White*
African American	78	25	18
Latino	8	50	13
White	14	25	69

Notes: Nonfatal violence includes aggravated and simple assault, rape or sexual assault, and robbery; African American and white categories exclude Latinos.

Source: Author's calculation from data in Morgan 2017.

Americans. Whites are thus 3.8 times more likely to be victimized by whites than by African Americans. Meanwhile, 78% of African American victims are victimized by other African Americans. Although only 50% of Latinos are victimized by other Latinos, Latinos are still twice as likely to be victimized by other Latinos than by either African Americans or whites.

A notable exception to the intraracial nature of criminal victimization involves Native Americans. In the NCVS report on their victimization discussed earlier, 88% of the violence against Native Americans was committed by African Americans or by whites. The same dynamic held true in the recent national survey evidence on the victimization of Native Americans by sexual violence and intimate-partner physical violence (Rosay 2016). The violent victimization of Native Americans is thus primarily interracial, while the victimization of other racial/and ethnic groups is primarily intraracial.

EXPLAINING RACIAL DIFFERENCES IN CRIMINAL VICTIMIZATION

Chapter 3 drew on explanations of crime to account for racial disparities in criminal behavior. Following this strategy, we now draw on explanations of criminal victimization to account for racial disparities in victimization. Explanations of criminal victimization try to answer two related questions: (1) Why are some people more likely than other people to be victimized? and (2) Why do some locations have higher victimization rates than others? Our brief discussion will help you understand criminal victimization in general, but its main purpose is to help you understand racial differences in victimization.

Explanations of criminal victimization highlight two sets of factors: (1) the *structural* factors that lead some locations, and thus the people living in them, to have higher victimization rates, and (2) the *individual* factors that lead some people to have higher victimization rates than other people within the same location.

Structural Factors and Criminal Victimization

Chapter 3 noted that structural factors explain why some people are more likely than others to commit crime, and why people of color are more likely to commit serious conventional crime. These factors include economic disadvantage and certain social and physical characteristics of communities. These same structural factors also explain why some people in general, and people of color in particular, are more likely to become crime victims. As Chapter 3 discussed, higher crime rates are found in urban neighborhoods with high rates of poverty, residential mobility, residential density, bars and taverns, and other problems. Because these types of settings have higher crime rates, people living in these settings are more likely to become crime victims than people living in more advantaged areas.

Criminological recognition of this fact increased with research findings that about 5% of all of a city's locations (street corners, intersections, residences, and businesses) account for at least 50% of all of that city's crime and victimization (Groff et al. 2015; Weisburd 2015). These high-crime locations are called **hot spots** of crime. Regardless of any precautions they may take, people living or working in or near these hot spots are more at risk for victimization. The structural factors that produce the higher crime rates in these locations also produce higher victimization risk in the locations.

The importance of residential density and certain other community characteristics for victimization rates reflects the assumptions of **routine activities theory**. According to this theory, criminal victimization is more likely to occur when three factors coincide: (1) the presence of *attractive targets*, which can be people or property; (2) the presence of a *motivated offender*(s); and (3) the absence of *guardianship*, or people or technology that might notice a potential victimization and help prevent it (Felson and Eckert 2016; Reyns et al. 2016). To illustrate this theory, one reason more robberies occur in areas with many bars and taverns (see Chapter 3) is that these businesses guarantee attractive targets in terms of people who carry money or credit cards and who might be too intoxicated to take precautions or to defend themselves. All things equal, then, locations with a greater concentration of bars and taverns will have higher victimization rates.

Relevance for Racial Differences in Victimization

Paralleling Chapter 3's discussion of racial differences in criminal behavior, a major reason for racial differences in victimization concerns where people tend to live. Simply put, African Americans and Latinos are much more likely than whites to live in the kinds of neighborhoods that, because of their mix of social and physical characteristics, have high crime rates. Just as people living in these neighborhoods are more at risk for committing crime, so are people living in these neighborhoods more at risk for being victimized by crime.

Sociologist Rodney Stark (1987:905–6) has observed that the higher crime rates of non-Southern African Americans are "the result of where they live . . . areas where the probability of *anyone* committing a crime are high" (emphasis his). These areas are the types of neighborhoods just outlined. The same observation applies to African Americans' higher victimization rates and also to Latinos' higher rates: Because African Americans and Latinos are so much more likely to live in these areas, they have higher victimization rates.

Physical location and economic disadvantage, then, help mightily to explain the higher victimization rates of people of color (Cancino,

Martinez, and Stowell 2009; Sampson 2013; Sampson and Lauritsen 1997). Although most research on this issue concerns African Americans and, to a smaller extent, Latinos, some research does highlight the importance of structural disadvantage for Native American victimization (Lanier and Huff-Corzine 2006).

Individual Factors and Criminal Victimization

Recall that it is also important to explain why some individuals are more likely than other individuals in the same locations to have higher victimization rates. Certain individual factors, then, also matter for criminal victimization in addition to the structural factors just discussed. One important individual factor is the regular behaviors that people follow. To be more precise, and drawing on **lifestyle theory**, some people have patterns of behavior—lifestyles—that increase their chances of become crime victims (Corkin et al. 2015). For example, people who often are at bars at night are more likely than people who stay home to become victims of assault or robbery. Those who have riskier lifestyles are more at risk for being victimized.

An especially risky lifestyle for being victimized involves committing crimes oneself or at least hanging out with people who commit crimes (Topalli, Wright, and Fornango 2002). The first activity just mentioned may bring someone into contact with other offenders and thus raises the risk of being victimized by them, while the second activity does involve such contact.

If people's lifestyles matter in all these ways, what influences their lifestyles? In particular, what influences them to engage either in a lifestyle riskier for victimization or instead in a safer lifestyle? Certain individual characteristics play a key role here.

One such characteristic is *low self-control* (Tillyer, Gialopsos, and Wilcox 2016; Turanovic, Reisig, and Pratt 2015). Persons with low-self control, often a result of inadequate parenting when they were children, are by definition more impulsive and less likely to plan their actions and to think about the potential consequences of their behavior. If so, they are also more likely to choose a riskier lifestyle or to otherwise put themselves into situations with the potential for criminal victimization.

A second characteristic involves *social relationships* (Franklin et al. 2012). Social relationships can either increase our chances of becoming victimized or decrease them. If we have friends who do drugs or otherwise get into trouble, these friendships may lead us to become victimized either by one of these friends or at least by one of their acquaintances, as our earlier discussion of lifestyle theory indicated. On the other hand, if our friends tend to be well behaved and certainly not the lawbreaking variety, we are less likely to become victimized. If, as a young adult, you are married or otherwise have strong family ties, you will probably be less likely to spend a lot of time away from home in bars and other settings that increase your chances of being victimized. If you have no such ties, you are more likely to engage in this type of riskier lifestyle and again to become a crime victim. Social relationships like those just listed all affect the potential for one's own criminal victimization, and they also help explain why some social categories have higher victimization rates. For example, males and young people have higher victimization rates than females and older people, respectively, partly because they are more apt than these latter two groups to associate with likely offenders (Chen 2009; Schreck 1999).

A third individual characteristic is a *history of childhood problems*, including child abuse and neglect and parental conflict (McIntyre and Widom 2011). Adolescents and adults with this history are more apt to have lower self-control, to have alcohol and other drug problems, to break the law, and to have low-quality social relationships. All of these factors in turn increase the potential for being victimized by crime.

Relevance for Racial Differences in Victimization

If risky lifestyles increase victimization, then one reason for the higher victimization rates of African Americans may be their greater involvement in certain risky lifestyles (Bunch, Clay-Warner, and Lei 2015; Peguero, Popp, and Koo 2015). One of these lifestyles is greater involvement in serious conventional crime, as documented in Chapter 3

(Madero-Hernandez and Fisher 2016). Although a small group of offenders largely accounts for this higher offending rate, this higher rate opens the door for offenders to be victimized by other offenders, driving up victimization rates for African Americans overall. This consequence reflects the idea that "demographic groups overrepresented in the population of offenders will be the most vulnerable to victimization because of their interaction with likely offenders" (Madero-Hernandez and Fisher 2016:5). Just as this dynamic helps explain the higher victimization rates of males and young people, it also helps explain the higher victimization rates of African Americans.

Although we might expect this dynamic to also explain the higher victimization rates of Latinos, the study of Chicago adolescents mentioned earlier found that Latino youths actually had less risky lifestyles than white adolescents, even though they had a higher victimization rate than white adolescents (Madero-Hernandez and Fisher 2016). The authors speculated that other factors might explain the Latino adolescents' higher victimization, including the idea that potential offenders may see them as easy targets because of their possible immigrant status.

Socioeconomic Status. Another reason for the higher victimization rates of African Americans and Latinos might be their socioeconomic status. Recall that victimization rates are higher among people who grew up in households with parental conflict, child abuse and neglect, and other problems, in part because these problems lead to risky lifestyles (Lee et al. 2012). Although it might sound like a stereotype, these problems are found more often in low-income households. Because African American families are much more likely to be poor or low-income, their various family problems may subject their children to greater risk for victimization as they grow older (Lee et al. 2012; Widom, Czaja and Dutton 2008). The same dynamic might hold true for Latino families and children, although some scholars think that Latino families tend to be resilient in the face of their economic situation (Martinez 2002; Steffensmeier et al. 2010).

Immigration. A study just discussed speculated that Latino youths' higher victimization rates may stem from perceptions concerning their immigrant status. Research does link some of the victimization of

Latinos and Asians in the United States both to the immigrant status that some of them enjoy and to offenders' beliefs, accurate or mistaken, that people of these backgrounds are immigrants. As a review of this research noted, "Immigrants, and especially undocumented immigrants, are highly vulnerable to violence, abuse, and exploitation" (Zatz and Smith 2012:146–47). Immigrants who are victimized may be afraid to call the police for fear of being deported, and because some offenders realize this sad fact, immigrants are "particularly attractive targets for victimization" (Zatz and Smith 2012:147). Offenders may also victimize immigrants because they simply hate immigrants and immigration. Also, many immigrants work as maids, day laborers, and other jobs in which they are vulnerable to financial exploitation and sexual and physical violence from their employers (Zatz and Smith 2012). All of these factors raise the victimization rates of immigrants—and probably also the racial and ethnic groups they represent.

Two Plausible Factors That Do Not Seem to Matter. Two additional factors that explain victimization should also conceivably help explain racial differences in victimization, but they do not appear to do so. The first such factor is *association with deviant peers.* In this way of thinking, youths living in high-crime areas should be more likely to have such peers simply because a greater number of individuals in these areas will be involved in illicit activities. These youths' associations with these peers should then subject them to a higher risk of criminal victimization. Because African American and Latino youths are more likely to live in high-crime areas, they should be more likely to have deviant peers and thus higher victimization rates.

Although this is a reasonable explanation, the Chicago study just discussed did not support it, because African American and Hispanic youths in the study both were not more likely than white youths to have deviant peers (Madero-Hernandez and Fisher 2016). In this regard, some national evidence suggests that white youths in fact are more likely to have deviant peers (Tillyer and Tillyer 2016). In view of this evidence, it is not clear that deviant peer relationships do help explain the racial differences in victimization.

Low self-control is the second plausible factor that does not appear to help explain racial differences in victimization. In this way of thinking, African American and Latino youths should have lower self-control than white youths because of their negative life circumstances and thus should be more likely to be victimized. However, national data on youths do not find racial/ethnic differences in low self-control (Tillyer and Tillyer 2016). Because low self-control does not appear to vary by race/ethnicity, it does not explain racial differences in victimization.

Summarizing Reasons for Racial Differences in Criminal Victimization

Racial differences in criminal victimization reflect the life circumstances in which the nation's racial and ethnic groups tend to live. Just as these circumstances lead to higher serious conventional crime rates for people of color, so do they lead to higher criminal victimization rates for people of color. These circumstances thus create a sort of "double whammy" for people of color. Whites are much more able to avoid this double whammy because they are much less likely to have the life circumstances conducive to crime and victimization. The research documenting these disparate situations leads criminologist Cassia Spohn (2011:326) to conclude that "racial and ethnic differences in victimization and offending rates can be attributed in large part to individual, family, and community characteristics. The sources of risk of victimization and offending are similar for all racial/ethnic groups, but the likelihood of experiencing these risk factors is higher for people of color than for whites."

WHY RACIAL DIFFERENCES IN CRIMINAL VICTIMIZATION ARE SIGNIFICANT

We have discussed and tried to explain racial differences in criminal victimization. These differences are significant for several reasons beyond just a general knowledge about them.

A first reason concerns the very fact that people of color are at greater risk for being victimized. Criminal victimization reflects the fault lines of

American society. As Chapter 1 emphasized, people of color are unequal in many ways, and their racial and ethnic inequality has profound negative consequences for many aspects of their lives. Their higher criminal victimization stems in large part from their inequality and also adds to it in a kind of vicious cycle. To the extent this is true, racial differences in victimization remind us of the damaging effects of racial and ethnic inequality and should spur efforts to reduce this inequality.

A second and related reason concerns the psychological, medical, economic, and behavioral consequences of being victimized. A rich body of research by criminologists, psychologists, sociologists, and medical researchers underscores the nature, extent, and impact of these consequences (Daigle 2018; Karmen 2016). Because criminal victimization is racially disproportionate, all of these consequences of victimization affect people of color more than non-Latino whites. These consequences include:

- Criminal victimization costs victims nearly $20 billion annually in direct costs (loss of money or property, immediate medical costs, lost wages) and perhaps hundreds of billions of dollars more in indirect costs (lost productivity, medical care for enduring mental and physical health problems, victim services, and so forth) (Miller, Cohen, and Wiersema 1996; Robinson and Rand 2011).
- Some crime victims suffer from anxiety, depression, loss of self-esteem, substance abuse problems, sleeplessness, suicidal tendencies, social relationship problems, and other issues (Orchowski and Gidycz 2015; Widom et al. 2013).
- *Indirect victimization* felt by relatives and friends of crime victims also occurs, as when people are bereaved by the death of a loved one from homicide.
- Children are also indirectly victimized when they hear gunshots or see violence actually occurring, as this *secondary exposure* to violence may impair their mental health and school performance (Badger and Ingraham 2016; Gibson, Morris, and Beaver 2009).

- Tragically, some crime victims become more likely to commit crime themselves because of their victimization, especially if it occurs during childhood or adolescence (Horan and Widom 2015).
- More generally, criminal victimization can generate fear in whole neighborhoods, keep people inside their residences, or prompt them to move away.

A final reason for the significance of racially disproportionate victimization brings us back to the discussion that began this chapter. To recall, a common view in news media coverage of crime and in the minds of the public and politicians is that white people are the primary victims of crime and that people of color prey on white people. This "fake truth" both reflects and fuels prejudice against people of color and may also increase support for harsher treatment of criminals at the various stages of the criminal justice system. The real truth is that people of color have higher victimization rates and that whites are largely victimized by other whites. If this real truth became widely known beyond the ranks of criminologists, their students, and other people who have studied these issues, perhaps racial prejudice and punitiveness would lessen, and perhaps criminal justice policy would be redirected away from the mass incarceration that has proven so costly in economic, human, and social terms. These might all be faint hopes, but our society owes it to people of color to move in this direction.

SUMMARY

1. African Americans, Latinos, and Native Americans have higher victimization rates than non-Latino whites. This difference is especially pronounced for homicide victimization when comparing African Americans and whites.
2. Structural and individual factors explain criminal victimization. Victimization is higher in disadvantaged areas because these areas' physical and social characteristics create opportunities for victimization. At the individual level, certain behaviors and lifestyles put people at more risk for being victimized.

3. People of color are more likely to live in disadvantaged areas, and the higher crime rates in those areas increase their residents' victimization rates.

4. Criminal victimization of African Americans, Latinos, and whites tends to be very intraracial; for Native Americans it tends to be interracial.

5. Racial differences in victimization reinforce the importance of reducing the racial inequality that helps generate these differences. They also underscore the fact that the many consequences of victimization affect people of color more often, and they show that the common perception of whites as victims attacked by African Americans is unfounded.

KEY TERMS

criminal victimization. The harming of people by conventional crime; some definitions would include harming by white-collar crime and other sources of harm

hot spots. Specific locations in cities with very high rates of crime and victimization

interracial. Regarding criminal victimization, the victimization of people of one race or ethnicity by people of another race or ethnicity

intraracial. Regarding criminal victimization, the idea that most victimization of African Americans, Latinos, and non-Latino whites is committed by people from their own race/ethnicity

lifestyle theory. The view that some people have lifestyles that increase their chances of becoming crime victims

routine activities theory. The view that criminal victimization is more likely to occur when three factors happen simultaneously: (1) the presence of attractive targets, which can be people or property; (2) the presence of a motivated offender(s); and (3) the absence of guardianship, or people or technology that might notice a potential victimization and help it not to occur

REFERENCES

Badger, Emily, and Christopher Ingraham. 2016. "How Violence Shapes Children for Life." *Washington Post* April 20. https://www.washingtonpost.com/news/wonk/wp/2016/04/20/how-violence-shapes-children-for-life/?post share=6431461245720956&tid=ss_tw-bottom

Bunch, Jackson, Jody Clay-Warner, and Man-Kit Lei. 2015. "Demographic Characteristics and Victimization Risk: Testing the Mediating Effects of Routine Activities." *Crime & Delinquency* 61:1181–205.

Bureau of Justice Statistics. 2017. "NCVS Victimization Analysis Tool." http://www.bjs.gov/index.cfm?ty=nvat.

Cancino, Jeffrey M., Ramiro Martinez, and Jacob I. Stowell. 2009. "The Impact of Neighborhood Context on Intragroup and Intergroup Robbery: The San Antonio Experience." *Annals of the American Academy of Political and Social Science* 623:12–24.

Chen, Xiaojin. 2009. "The Linkage Between Deviant Lifestyles and Victimization: An Examination from a Life Course Perspective." *Journal of Interpersonal Violence* 24(7):1083–110.

Corkin, Danya, Margit Wiesner, Ronda S. Reyna, and Kathan Shukla. 2015. "The Role of Deviant Lifestyles on Violent Victimization in Multiple Contexts." *Deviant Behavior* 36(5):405–28.

Daigle, Leah E. 2018. *Victimology: The Essentials.* Thousand Oaks, CA: Sage.

Federal Bureau of Investigation. 2017. *Crime in the United States, 2016.* Washington, DC: Federal Bureau of Investigation.

Felson, Marcus, and Mary Eckert. 2016. *Crime and Everyday Life.* Thousand Oaks, CA: Sage.

Franklin, Cortney A., Travis W. Franklin, Matt R. Nobles, and Glen A. Kercher. 2012. "Assessing the Effect of Routine Activity Theory and Self-Control on Property, Personal, and Sexual Assault Victimization." *Criminal Justice & Behavior* 39(10):1296–315.

Gibson, Chris L., Sara Z. Morris, and Kevin M. Beaver. 2009. "Secondary Exposure to Violence during Childhood and Adolescence: Does Neighborhood Context Matter?" *JQ: Justice Quarterly* 26(1):30–57.

Groff, Elizabeth R., Jerry H. Ratcliffe, Cory P. Haberman, Evan T. Sorg, Nola M. Joyce, and Ralph B. Taylor. 2015. "Does What Police Do at Hot Spots Matter? The Philadelphia Policing Tactics Experiment." *Criminology* 53(1):23–53.

Horan, Jacqueline M., and Cathy Spatz Widom. 2015. "Cumulative Childhood Risk and Adult Functioning in Abused and Neglected Children Grown Up." *Development & Psychopathology* 27(3):927–41.

Karmen, Andrew. 2016. *Crime Victims: An Introduction to Victimology.* Belmont, CA: Cengage.

Kim, Sangmoon, Cecil L. Willis, Keely Latterner, and Randy LaGrange. 2016. "When Birds of a Feather Don't Flock Together: A Macrostructural Approach to Interracial Crime." *Sociological Inquiry* 86(2):166–88.

Lanier, Christina, and Lin Huff-Corzine. 2006. "American Indian Homicide: A County-Level Analysis Utilizing Social Disorganization Theory." *Homicide Studies* 10:181–94.

Lee, Chioun, Courtney Cronley, Helene Raskin White, Eun-Young Mun, Magda Stouthamer-Loeber, and Rolf Loeber. 2012. "Racial Differences in the Consequences of Childhood Maltreatment for Adolescent and Young Adult Depression, Heavy Drinking, and Violence." *Journal of Adolescent Health* 50(5):443–49.

Madero-Hernandez, Arelys, and Bonnie S. Fisher. 2016. "Race, Ethnicity, Risky Lifestyles, and Violent Victimization: A Test of a Mediation Model." *Race and Justice.* DOI: 10.1177/2153368716651476.

Martinez, Ramiro, Jr. 2002. *Latino Homicide: Immigration, Violence, and Community.* New York: Routledge.

McIntyre, Jared Kean, and Cathy Spatz Widom. 2011. "Childhood Victimization and Crime Victimization." *Journal of Interpersonal Violence* 26(4):640–63.

Miller, Ted, Marc Cohen, and Brian Wiersema. 1996. *Victim Costs and Consequences: A New Look.* Washington, DC: National Institute of Justice, U.S. Department of Justice.

Morgan, Rachel E. 2017. *Race and Hispanic Origin of Victims and Offenders, 2012-15.* Washington, DC: Bureau of Justice Statistics, U.S. Department of Justice.

Orchowski, Lindsay M., and Christine A. Gidycz. 2015. "Psychological Consequences Associated with Positive and Negative Responses to Disclosure of Sexual Assault among College Women: A Prospective Study." *Violence Against Women* 21(7):803–23.

Peguero, Anthony A., Ann Marie Popp, and Dixie J. Koo. 2015. "Race, Ethnicity, and School-Based Adolescent Victimization." *Crime & Delinquency* 61:323–49.

Perry, Steven W. 2004. *American Indians and Crime: A BJS Statistical Profile, 1992–2002.* Washington, DC: Bureau of Justice Statistics, U.S. Department of Justice.

Reyns, Bradford W., Billy Henson, Bonnie S. Fisher, Kathleen A. Fox, and Matt R. Nobles. 2016. "A Gendered Lifestyle-Routine Activity Approach to Explaining Stalking Victimization in Canada." *Journal of Interpersonal Violence* 31(9):1719–43.

Robinson, Jayne E., and Michael R. Rand. 2011. *Criminal Victimization in the United States, 2008—Statistical Tables.* Washington, DC: Bureau of Justice Statistics, U.S. Department of Justice

Rosay, André B. 2016. *Violence Against American Indian and Alaska Native Women and Men: 2010 Findings From the National Intimate Partner and Sexual Violence Survey* Washington, DC: National Institute of Justice.

Sampson, Robert J. 2013. *Great American City: Chicago and the Enduring Neigh-borhood Effect*. Chicago: University of Chicago Press.

Sampson, Robert J., and Janet L. Lauritsen. 1997. "Racial and Ethnic Disparities in Crime and Criminal Justice in the United States." *Crime and Justice: A Review of Research* 19:311–74.

Schreck, Christopher J. 1999. "Criminal Victimization and Low Self-Control: An Extension and Test of a General Theory of Crime." *Justice Quarterly* 16:633–54.

Semega, Jessica L., Kayla R. Fontenot, and Melissa A. Kollar. 2017. *Income and Poverty in the United States: 2016*. Washington, DC: U.S. Census Bureau.

Spohn, Cassia. 2011. "Race, Ethnicity, and Crime." In *The Oxford Handbook of Crime and Criminal Justice*, edited by Michael Tonry, 321–47. New York: Oxford University Press.

Stark, Rodney. 1987. "Deviant Places: A Theory of the Ecology of Crime." *Criminology* 25:893–911.

Steffensmeier, Darrell, Jeffery T. Ulmer, B. E. N. Feldmeyer, and Casey T. Harris. 2010. "Scope and Conceptual Issues in Testing the Race-Crime Invariance Thesis: Black, White, and Hispanic Comparisons." *Criminology* 48(4):1133–69.

Tillyer, Marie Skubak, Brooke Miller Gialopsos, and Pamela Wilcox. 2016. "The Short-Term Repeat Sexual Victimization of Adolescents in School." *Crime & Delinquency* 62(1):81–106.

Tillyer, Marie, and Rob Tillyer. 2016. "Race, Ethnicity, and Adolescent Violent Victimization." *Journal of Youth & Adolescence* 45(7):1497–511.

Topalli, Volkan, Richard Wright, and Robert Fornango. 2002. "Drug Dealers, Robbery and Retaliation: Vulnerability, Deterrence and the Contagion of Violence." *British Journal of Criminology* 42:337–51.

Turanovic, Jillian, Michael Reisig, and Travis Pratt. 2015. "Risky Lifestyles, Low Self-Control, and Violent Victimization Across Gendered Pathways to Crime." *Journal of Quantitative Criminology* 31(2):183–206.

Weisburd, David. 2015. "The Law of Crime Concentration and the Criminology of Place." *Criminology* 53(2):133–57.

Widom, Cathy Spatz, Sally J. Czaja, and Mary Ann Dutton. 2008. "Childhood Victimization and LIfetime Revictimization." *Child Abuse & Neglect* 32(8):785–96.

Widom, Cathy Spatz, Sally Czaja, Helen W. Wilson, Maureen Allwood, and Preeti Chauhan. 2013. "Do the Long-Term Consequences of Neglect Differ for Children of Different Races and Ethnic Backgrounds?" *Child Maltreat-ment* 18(1):42–55.

Zatz, Marjorie S., and Hilary Smith. 2012. "Immigration, Crime, and Victimiza-tion: Rhetoric and Reality." *Annual Review of Law & Social Science* 8(1):141–59.

[5]

RACE AND POLICING

Chapter Outline

Learning Questions

1. How does the history of the criminal justice system reflect racism in the South and elsewhere?
2. How does the focal concerns perspective explain possible racial/ethnic bias in criminal justice?
3. What is the evidence that indicates racial profiling in police stops and searches?

4. What does a recent systematic review of research on race and arrest conclude?
5. Does racial bias appear to motivate police use of force? What is the evidence for and against this assumption?

This chapter is the first of two chapters to examine possible racial discrimination in the criminal justice system. We focus on policing in this chapter and on prosecution and punishment in the next chapter. Our discussion here of policing begins with some important history.

REMEMBERING THE PAST

Before the 1970s and 1980s, the criminal justice system in many parts of the United States served as a weapon for white supremacists to oppress and terrorize African Americans. This nightmare typified the U.S. South and also areas outside the South. The police back then harassed African Americans with impunity and arrested them routinely on trumped-up charges. These "suspects" would then stay in jail without benefit of counsel and be at the mercy of white guards and inmates. Those whose cases came to trial would quickly be convicted by white judges or all-white juries. If then sentenced to jail or prison, these inmates had to endure squalid living conditions and renewed abuse from white guards and inmates (Browne-Marshall 2013; Myrdal 1944).

This was the era of virulent **Jim Crow racism**, when whites in the South and elsewhere held appalling views about race. Because criminal justice personnel in these areas also held these views, it is not surprising that law enforcement, courts, and jails and prisons all served as vehicles to help keep African Americans "in their place."

This situation began during the slavery era, when the criminal justice system as we know it today was just beginning. Law enforcement agents called *slave patrollers* captured escaped slaves and enforced the notorious Southern *slave codes*, which prevented slaves from becoming literate and sharply regulated all other aspects of their lives (Russell-Brown 2009).

After the Civil War, the vile *Black Codes* greatly restricted the lives of freed slaves and in particular allowed law enforcement agents to arrest them on false grounds and send them to prison. Meanwhile, Northerners after the Civil War and well into the twentieth century viewed African Americans as a dangerous species that needed to be imprisoned to keep white society safe. Police forces grew accordingly (Muhammad 2011).

This widespread effort to control black people motivated much of the development of American criminal justice during the nineteenth and early twentieth centuries. As law professor Bryan Stevenson (2017:11) observes, "Before the end of the nineteenth century, states looked to the criminal justice system to construct policies and strategies to maintain white supremacy and racial subordination. Law enforcement officers were tasked with menacing and controlling black people in ways that would shape policing and the criminal justice system in America for the next century."

Against this historical backdrop, the deliberate use of criminal justice before the 1970s to preserve white dominance was just business as usual. Fortunately, this situation began to change, thanks to the 1960s civil rights movement and to legal reforms produced by federal legislation and U.S. Supreme Court rulings (Browne-Marshall 2013). Meanwhile, the Jim Crow racism of the pre–civil rights era gradually gave way to the unconscious racial prejudice and stereotyping today that is called *implicit bias* (see Chapter 2). As this chapter and the next chapter will show, if the Jim Crow racism of the past motivated the cruel use of the criminal justice system against African Americans, today's implicit bias now underlies a less cruel and less obvious pattern of racial/ethnic discrimination in the criminal justice system (Levinson and Smith 2012). Even if this pattern of discrimination is less severe, it is still very harmful.

PREVIEWING THE DISCUSSION

This chapter examines the evidence that points to this pattern of discrimination for policing, while the next chapter examines the evidence for prosecution and sentencing. In examining all of this evidence, these two chapters return to a key question presented in Chapter 1: To what extent do racial disparities in criminal justice reflect actual racial differences in offending versus racial discrimination by the criminal justice system? The following discussion provides a framework for interpreting the evidence that these next two chapters will discuss.

Understanding Racial/Ethnic Discrimination in Criminal Justice

Scholars dispute the extent of discrimination in today's criminal justice system. Judging from debate over the past few decades, their views range from the idea that a racist criminal justice system in the post–civil rights era is just a "myth" (Wilbanks 1987) to the idea that criminal justice is still racist and still a rather deliberate means for repressing people of color (Butler 2017; Mann 1993). In between these polar opposites is a *middle-ground view* that we have already stated and that will guide our discussion of the research evidence. This view sees racial and ethnic discrimination as continuing in the criminal justice system but as largely unintended and less blatant than in the Jim Crow era.

This middle-ground view reflects a **focal concerns perspective**. According to this perspective, racial discrimination in criminal justice stems from implicit biases and racial stereotypes that assume people of color, and especially young African American males, are prone to violent crime (Levinson and Smith 2012; Steffensmeier, Painter-Davis, and Ulmer 2017). Law professor Katheryn Russell-Brown (2009) calls this latter presumption the *criminalblackman* stereotype. As she (2015:133) puts it, "For most people the idea of crime brings to mind images of black faces, and . . . images of black faces bring to mind thoughts of crime." Law professor Paul Butler (2017:9) agrees: "Let's keep it real. Many people—cops, politicians, and ordinary people—see African American men as a threat."

This presumption of danger from young males of color creates for police and other criminal justice professionals a "perceptual shorthand" that shapes how they deal with these males (Gau and Jordan 2015). In particular, it may lead them to treat suspects and defendants of color more harshly in various ways, as these next two chapters will demonstrate.

Similarly, because these professionals tend to view non-Latino whites as less dangerous and more respectable, they may treat white suspects and defendants less severely, and they may also treat suspects and defendants in cases with white victims more severely.

Scholars who hold the middle-ground view assume that most criminal justice professionals do not consciously intend to discriminate against people of color in all of the ways just described. Some of these professionals may be out-and-out racists, but most are not. Instead, these professionals act in a discriminatory manner without necessarily realizing they are doing so (Spohn 2015).

Implicit Bias and Entrenched Discrimination

How is this possible? As Chapter 2 noted, the concept of implicit bias means that many people hold stereotypes about race and ethnicity without being aware they are biased. Criminal justice professionals are no different. In fact, national survey evidence finds that white police officers are nine times more likely than white civilians to think African Americans are more violent than whites (LeCount 2017). To acknowledge that any discrimination criminal justice professionals commit is usually unintended is not meant to excuse their behavior, but it is meant to acknowledge that well-intentioned people may still sometimes act in a wrongheaded manner.

Many scholars emphasize that this discrimination is not easy to eliminate. It is bad enough, they say, that many criminal justice professionals are implicitly biased, but it is even worse that this discrimination is largely entrenched in the criminal justice system, given its historical development to repress African Americans (Butler 2017; A. Davis 2017). As law professor Butler (2017:17) argues, "The most problematic practices of American criminal justice—excessive force by police, harsh sentencing, the erosion of civil liberties, widespread government surveillance, and mass incarceration—are best understood as measures originally intended for African American men." To these scholars, policing and other aspects of criminal justice today are accomplishing, even if more benignly, what Jim Crow accomplished in the past: the repression of African Americans, especially African American men. As law professor Michelle Alexander (2012:4) puts it, today's criminal justice system is "a stunningly comprehensive and well-disguised system of racialized social control that functions in a manner strikingly similar to Jim Crow."

Focusing on Police and Policing

With this framework in mind, we will now discuss the research evidence on race and policing. Alleged examples over the years of police harassment, brutality, and other misconduct have created serious rifts between police and people of color. To the extent that police do mistreat people of color, they are failing many members of our society and prompting them to mistrust and fear police much more than white Americans do (Weitzer, Tuch, and Skogan 2008).

Two U.S. Department of Justice investigations during the past decade found that some police departments have exhibited a deplorable pattern of racial bias. One of these investigations focused on Ferguson, Missouri, where a police shooting of an African American male in 2014 aroused national controversy and protest (discussed later). In response, the Justice Department investigated the Ferguson Police Department and concluded that it had been arresting or citing African Americans so often that it was routinely violating their constitutional rights (Apuzzo 2015). This pattern of police behavior included the use of excessive force.

The second Justice Department investigation concerned police in Baltimore, Maryland. Prompted by the 2015 death in a police wagon of an African American male (discussed later), the investigation concluded that the Baltimore Police Department had "engaged in years of racially discriminatory policing that targeted black residents, illegally detaining and searching people and using excessive force," according to a news report (Hermann, Bui, and Zapotosky 2016). The report said that police also strip-searched some people in public, and that police supervisors had told patrol officers to target African Americans.

Are the Baltimore and Ferguson Police Departments typical, or are they the exception? Does the evidence support the indictment of policing by many commentators? To try to answer this question, we will examine the evidence for several aspects of policing from police jurisdictions around the nation. Some police departments such as those in Baltimore and Ferguson are worse than others in their treatment of people of color, and some are better. Please keep this variability in mind as you read about the research evidence.

RACE AND STOPS AND SEARCHES

In interviews by journalists and researchers, young African American males report being routinely stopped by police while walking down the street (*street stops*) or driving a motor vehicle (*traffic stops*), when all they are doing is walking or driving (Brunson 2007; Rios 2015; Stewart 2007). The sarcastic terms *WWB* ("walking while black") and *DWB* ("driving while black") have entered the national lexicon as the reasons for many of these stops.

The police are, of course, authorized to stop drivers and pedestrians they deem suspicious, as long as they have reasonable grounds for their suspicion. U.S. Supreme Court rulings allow police to take race into account when they decide whom to stop, as long as race is not the only factor that prompts a stop (Hutchins 2017). Still, if police stop civilians in part because of a civilian's race or ethnicity, they are nonetheless engaging in **racial profiling**, or the assumption that someone's race or ethnicity indicates greater potential for criminal behavior (Hutchins 2017). This is true whether or not police consciously realize they are considering race when they make a stop.

Research on racial profiling involves three related dimensions. A first line of research compares the racial/ethnic proportions of people who are stopped with the racial/ethnic proportions of the population in the study location (a specific city, county, or state). A second line of research compares the racial/ethnic percentages of stopped civilians who then have their vehicles and/or persons searched. Meanwhile, a third line of research compares the racial/ethnic percentages of searches that uncover illegal contraband (drugs, weapons, etc.). The results of all this research may be summarized as follows (Glaser 2015; Spohn 2011):

1. The first line of research generally finds that people of color are indeed disproportionately stopped while driving or walking.

2. The second line of research finds that when people of color are stopped, they are more likely than stopped whites to be searched.

3. The third line of research finds that once searched, people of color are either (depending on the study) no more likely, or even less likely, than whites to possess illegal contraband.

Selected Studies of Racial Profiling

A few examples will help illustrate this set of results:

- In one of the first studies of racial profiling, African American drivers on the New Jersey Turnpike in the late 1990s comprised 42% of all traffic stops even though they comprised only 15% of all turnpike drivers (Hutchins 2017).

- In Baltimore County, Maryland, African Americans comprise 50% of all traffic stops, even though they comprise only 27% of county residents; they are also more likely than stopped white drivers to be searched, but less likely to be found with illegal contraband. These trends also hold true for other areas of Maryland (Rector 2016).

- In Connecticut, African Americans comprise 14% of all traffic stops, even though they comprise only 9% of Connecticut's population. This general racial disparity was found to be larger during daytime, when officers can more easily perceive a driver's race before pulling the driver over, than at nighttime, a difference that strongly suggests racial profiling (Soffen 2016).

- In various cities in Connecticut, Illinois, North Carolina, and Rhode Island, stopped African American drivers are 1.5 times to 5.2 times more likely, depending on the city and state, than stopped white drivers to have their vehicles searched, but are less likely to be found with illegal contraband when searched (LaFraniere and Lehren 2015).

- In Vermont, African American and Latino drivers are several times more likely than white drivers to be stopped, even though they are less likely to be found with illegal contraband after being searched (M. Davis 2017).

- During the early 2000s, New York City police conducted hundreds of thousands of street stops yearly. Some 83% of these stopped civilians were African American or Latino, even though these two groups account for only about 50% of New York's population. Almost 90% of these street stops did not prompt an arrest, and there were no racial differences in arrest after being stopped. These circumstances meant there were no grounds for the racial disparity in the street stops, a federal judge later declared. Saying that the policy involved routine stops of "blacks and Hispanics who would not have been stopped if they were white," the judge ruled that the policy was unconstitutional (Goldstein 2013:A1).

- In national survey evidence for the 2002-2011 period, 9.4% of African Americans who had some contact with the police (during traffic or street stops or as suspects, victims, witnesses, and persons in need) during the past year reported being searched, compared to 3.6% of Latinos and 2.8% of non-Latino whites (Hyland, Langton and Davis 2015). Although these differences demonstrate racial disparity in police searches, this survey yielded no evidence of racial disparities in traffic or street stops, as the percentages of both types of stops involving African Americans or Latinos did not exceed these groups' respective shares of the national population (Hyland, Langton and Davis 2015).

Racial Profiling or Only Racial Disparity?

The examples just presented do not necessarily prove that racial profiling occurs in police stops and searches. To play devil's advocate, perhaps people of color drive more miles than whites and thus have more traffic violations simply because they drive more often (Soffen 2016). Similarly, perhaps people of color have worse driving habits than whites and experience more frequent traffic stops for this reason (Tillyer and Engel 2012). Perhaps their more frequent searches after traffic stops reflect the fact that traffic officers' criminal record checks using their vehicles' online computer systems are more likely to disclose a criminal record for people of color than for whites (Tillyer 2014).

Exploring the driving habit possibility further, some research does find that people of color are more likely to speed while driving, to use their cell phones, to not use seat belts, and otherwise to have worse driving habits (Lundman and Kowalski 2009; Tillyer and Engel 2012), as unlikely as that might sound. If so, this evidence suggests that racial disparities in traffic stops may not, in fact, stem entirely from racial profiling. Although research finds that a greater history of criminal records also helps explain why people of color are more likely to be searched after a traffic stop, it finds that this disparity persists even after this variable is taken into account (Tillyer 2014). This latter finding strongly suggests racial profiling in traffic stop searches, a pattern that is also suggested by the fact that searched people of color are no more likely, as we have seen, to be found with illegal contraband. Overall, then, the evidence on police stops and searches does point to racial profiling in areas across the United States, but more research is needed on the extent of this profiling.

Race and Arrest

Chapter 3 concluded that racial/ethnic differences in serious offending help explain the higher arrest rates for people of color. Do police racial biases also account for this arrest disparity? Are people of color more likely than whites who commit the same crimes to be arrested?

Before examining the evidence, it is worth noting that the police have great *discretion* regarding arrest, as they do with street and traffic stops. Simply put, they can decide to arrest someone who has apparently committed a crime, or they can decide not to arrest that person. In fact, they actually decide not to arrest many people they could have arrested (Dempsey and Forst 2016). Such discretion opens the door for race and ethnicity and other extralegal factors to affect whom police officers decide to arrest or not to arrest.

Evidence on Race and Arrest

Research on possible racial bias in arrest yields some inconsistent evidence. A notable study in the 1960s involved trained observers riding around in police cars (Black 1980). This study found that police were more likely to arrest African American suspects than white suspects, but it concluded that this disparity was due to factors other than police racial bias. These factors were: (1) African Americans were suspected of more serious crimes overall than white suspects; (2) African American suspects were more hostile than white suspects toward police; and (3) victims tended to prefer arrest more often when suspects were African American than when they were white. Some other observational studies also find that these factors explain why police are more likely to arrest African American suspects (Riksheim and Chermak 1993). Although the police might be on their best behavior when they know they are being observed, these studies still suggest that arrest is not racially motivated.

Complicating the picture, other research does find racial bias in arrest, especially when the crime victim is white (Smith, Visher, and Davidson 1984), and especially for misdemeanor offenses when police practice "zero-tolerance policing" aimed at clearing the streets of minor offenders (Rosenfeld, Fornango, and Rengifo 2007). The mixed findings on this issue prompted two expert reviews to conclude a decade or more ago that the evidence overall on racial bias in arrest was inconclusive (Rosich 2007; Skogan and Frydl 2004).

However, a more recent systematic review drew a firmer conclusion. Taking into account nonracial factors, such as the seriousness of the crime, that can affect arrest, the review found that the average probability of arrest for minority suspects in the studies it examined was 26%, compared to only 20% for white suspects (Kochel, Wilson, and Mastrofski 2011). Doing a little math, minority suspects were thus 30% more likely than white suspects to be arrested. Calling this "a strong and strikingly consistent pattern of race effects" (475), the review's authors asserted, "From our findings, we can conclude more definitively than prior nonsystematic reviews that racial minority suspects experience a higher probability of arrest than do Whites. We report with confidence that the results are not mixed. Race matters" (498).

Two other types of racial bias may also influence the chance of arrest. One type involves the *strength of the evidence*: Some research finds that African American and Latino suspects are more likely than white suspects to be arrested when the evidence of a crime is fairly weak, while white suspects tend not to be arrested unless the evidence is fairly strong (Hagan and Zatz 1985; Petersilia 1983). The second type involves *skin tone*: Some research finds that white men with darker skin are more likely to be arrested than lighter-skinned white men, with skin tone making no difference for black men's arrests (Branigan et al. 2017). Chapter 6 will discuss the evidence on skin tone and sentencing.

Race and Arrest for Drug Offenses

Evidence of racial/ethnic discrimination in arrest is especially pronounced in arrests for drug offenses. As Chapters 1 and 3 pointed out, African Americans and, to a smaller extent, Latinos are disproportionally arrested for drug offenses (possession or sale) even though they are not more likely than Anglos to use or sell illegal drugs (Spohn 2015). The war against drugs, then, has been very racially discriminatory. Chapter 6 returns to this issue further in the context of prosecution and sentencing for drug offenses.

RACE AND POLICE USE OF FORCE

In February 2012, George Zimmerman, a neighborhood watch volunteer for a gated community in Sanford, Florida, killed Trayvon Martin, a 17-year-old African American male. Zimmerman confronted Martin when he saw him walking, unarmed, from a convenience store to the gated community, where he was visiting his father's fiancée. A fight broke out that ended with Zimmerman fatally shooting Martin. It is widely assumed that Zimmerman was suspicious of Martin simply because Martin was an African American who was wearing a hoodie (Blow 2012). Zimmerman's jury acquittal in July 2013 set off protests across the United States and prompted the founding of the Black Lives Matter movement. It also led President Barack Obama to observe that black men were often the targets of racial profiling and that "Trayvon Martin could have been me 35 years ago" (Landler and Shear 2013:A1).

Although Zimmerman was not a sworn police officer, many African Americans have died from police shootings and other police actions since

Martin's killing. These incidents often aroused national attention, strong criticism, and local and sometimes national protests. Examples include the following:

- In July 2014, Eric Garner, an unarmed 42-year-old African American male, died in New York City from a police chokehold. Garner was allegedly selling cigarettes illegally when a police officer tried to arrest him. When Garner pulled his arm away from being hand-cuffed, the officer grabbed him in a chokehold, shoved his head face down on the ground, and kept him in that position. Garner said "I can't breathe" eleven times, lost consciousness, and later died at a hospital. The officer was not prosecuted (Baker, Goodman, and Muellerjune 2015).

- In August 2014, a white police officer in Ferguson, Missouri, fatally shot Michael Brown, an unarmed 18-year-old African American male whom the officer had stopped as a suspect in a convenience store robbery. Some witnesses said Brown had his hands up in surrender when he was shot. Mass protests erupted in Ferguson, but the U.S. Department of Justice investigation discussed earlier in this chapter concluded that there was not enough evidence to prosecute the officer (Eckholm and Apuzzo 2015).

- In April 2015, a police officer fatally shot Walter Scott, an unarmed 33-year-old African American male, in North Charleston, South Carolina, after stopping him for a broken car brake light. After a confrontation, Scott fled, and the officer shot him from behind eight times, with three bullets hitting Scott in the back, one in his ear, and one in his backside. The officer's murder trial ended in a deadlocked jury, but he later pleaded guilty to federal charges of violating Scott's civil rights (Blinder 2017).

- Also in April 2015, Freddie Gray, a 25-year-old African American male, died in Baltimore, Maryland, of a broken neck, presumably sustained while being transported in a police van, after being arrested for allegedly carrying an illegal switchblade. A prosecutor later said Gray was in fact carrying a legal knife, and witnesses reported that the arresting officers had brutalized Gray during his arrest, including shoving a knee into his neck. The six police officers involved in the arrest and transport were later prosecuted on various charges and tried separately. After one trial ended in a deadlocked jury and three trials ended in a judge's acquittal, prosecutors dropped all remaining charges (Fenton 2017; McDonell-Parry and Barron 2017).

- In July 2016, a police officer fatally shot Philando Castile, a 32-year-old male African American, in a St. Paul, Minnesota, suburb. The officer and his partner had pulled over Castile and his girlfriend in a traffic stop. Although Castile reportedly told the officer that he was legally armed, he was shot even though he was not reaching for his gun. A jury acquitted the officer of all charges in June 2017, but the city fired him a day later. Castile's mother said after the acquittal, "My son loved this city and this city killed my son. And the murderer gets away. Are you kidding me right now?" (Berman 2017).

- In September 2016, a police officer fatally shot Terence Crutcher, an unarmed 40-year-old African American male, in Tulsa, Oklahoma. Crutcher had walked with his hands up to the driver's side of his car that he had left in the middle of a road and was shot as he stood beside the car. The officer said later that Crutcher had been reaching inside his car, but police videos suggested that the driver's window was closed (Eaton and Kaleem 2016). A jury later acquitted the officer of first-degree manslaughter (Walinchus and Pérez-Peña 2017).

- In March 2018, two police officers investigating a vandalism complaint fatally shot Stephon Clark, an unarmed 22-year-old African American male, in his grandmother's backyard in Sacramento, California. An autopsy commissioned by Clark's family found he had been shot eight times from the back. The officers said they feared Clark had a gun, but the only object found on his body was his cell phone (Robles and Del Real 2018).

These were just seven of the many deaths of African Americans from police use of force during the past few years. Police, of course, are authorized to use lethal and nonlethal force if necessary, and they often have to do so to defend their own lives and safety or those of civilians. But many police shootings appear to be unnecessary, even though prosecutors and grand juries routinely decline to bring charges against police for these shootings, and even though judges or trial juries just as routinely find them not guilty when they are prosecuted and tried (Fairfax 2017; Smith, Alcindor, and Healy 2017).

A Continuing Concern

Police use of force (also called *police violence*) has long been a major concern among people of color and is a major source of their dissatisfaction with the police (see Chapter 2). During the 1960s, many U.S. cities experienced urban riots in which most of the participants were African Americans. President Johnson's commission on the riots, discussed in Chapter 1, later blamed police brutality against African Americans as a major reason for them (Kerner Commission 1968).

Urban unrest occurred again in the wake of the notorious police beating of Rodney King in July 1991. Several Los Angeles police officers beat King, a 25-year-old African American male, after a high-speed car chase, hitting him more than 30 times with their batons and also kicking him. A neighbor's videotape of the beating that was sent to a local TV station soon captured nationwide attention. The jury acquittal of three of the officers the following April prompted six days of rioting in Los Angeles and also riots in some other cities. A federal jury later found two of the officers guilty for violating King's civil rights (Cannon 1998).

King's beating was not an aberration, as many other African Americans sustain excessive force by police, even if their incidents do not receive the publicity that King's beating did (Henning 2017). Young African American males in urban areas feel they routinely confront the possibility of police violence whenever they are out in public (Butler 2017; Rios 2015). This situation prompts African American parents to teach their sons from an early age how to behave in the presence of police so as to minimize the use of police force. As law professor Kristin Henning (2017:64) states, "Black parents tell their children to 'always keep your hands where they can see them,' 'avoid sudden movements,' and 'behave in a courteous and respectful manner toward officers.'"

Evidence on Race and Police Use of Force

Is police use of force racially discriminatory? Social scientists have long been concerned about this possibility, with one scholar famously concluding that "police have one trigger finger for whites and another for blacks" (Takagi 1974:30).

There is indeed ready evidence of racial disparity in police shootings. The police annually kill about 1,000 civilians, most of them armed, in the line of duty; about half of these civilians are African American or Latino (Kelly et al. 2016). Because African Americans and Latinos together comprise only about 31% of the U.S. population, the number of killed African Americans and Latinos represents a racial disparity. Adjusting for population size, African Americans are three times more likely than whites to be killed by police (Kelly et al. 2016). Although African American males represent only 6% of the U.S. population, they comprise 34% of deaths from police shootings of unarmed civilians (Kelly et al. 2016). Relatedly, 13% of African Americans who die from a police shooting are unarmed, compared to only 7% of whites who die from a police shooting (Lowery 2016). But do all these racial disparities reflect racial bias? In terms of research, this is a difficult question to answer for several reasons.

First, reliable data on police use of force are sorely lacking (Klinger et al. 2016). About as twice as many civilians die annually from police shootings than the number estimated by the FBI and National Vital Statistics System. The *Washington Post,* the *Guardian*, and other parties have compiled listings of many more fatal shootings by police, and researchers are using their databases to study these shootings (Nix et al. 2017); the racial disparity data in police shootings just discussed come from these databases. But because these databases rely on media accounts of the shootings, their information is incomplete (Klinger and Slocum 2017).

Second, even if reliable data for fatal shootings were available, there are no reliable data for nonfatal shootings by police. This is an important problem because most police shootings do not result in a civilian's death: Civilians are actually struck by bullets in only about one-third to one-half of police shootings, and they die in only about one-third of the time when struck (Klinger et al. 2016). Putting these numbers together, civilians die only about 9%–17% of the time when police try to shoot them. Data for police use of force that does not involve a shooting are even less reliable, because police do not usually report these incidents, and victims often fear doing so.

Third, even if data show that people of color are more likely to experience police use of force, this might occur because they might more often commit serious violent crime and thus are more often confronted by police as suspects. Regarding this possibility, because African Americans and Latinos together account for about 60% of violent crime arrests (see Chapter 3), some observers say this high percentage helps explain why these two groups also account for so many civilians killed by police (Miller et al. 2017). African Americans' overrepresentation in police violence may also reflect the possibility that they may be more likely to resist arrest (Reisig et al. 2004), or the fact that police more heavily patrol high-crime urban areas populated by African Americans. All of these possibilities suggest that evidence of racial disparity in police use of force may not actually reflect police racial bias in the decision to use force.

Implicit Bias and Use of Force

There is reason to suspect that police officers' implicit racial bias does motivate their use of force (Harris 2015; Russell-Brown 2017). Some research on implicit bias shows subjects (civilians or police, depending on the study) photographs or videos that depict African American and white men holding either a gun or another object such as a cell phone or wallet (Correll et al. 2007; Plant and Peruche 2005; Sadler et al. 2012). The subjects are asked to press a "shoot" button if the man is armed or a "don't shoot" button if he is unarmed. The exact findings depend on the particular study, but overall this research finds that subjects are more likely to shoot armed black men than armed white men, and to do so more quickly, and also more likely to shoot unarmed black men than unarmed white men. However, one simulated study found that police were less likely to "shoot" African American suspects and to take a longer time to "shoot" them, perhaps because its police subjects were concerned about being perceived as racist if they shoot minority suspects (James, James, and Vila 2016). These inconsistencies underscore the difficulty of understanding why racial disparities in actual police use of force occur.

Examining the Evidence

So what does the real-life evidence say? Most research on race and police violence analyzes quantitative data on police fatal shootings. This research sometimes finds that police fatal shootings are more frequent in locations with higher proportions of African American residents, even when these areas' crime rates are taken into account (Jacobs and Britt 1979; Jacobs and O'Brien 1998). A study of this type involving U.S. counties found that unarmed African Americans were 3.49 times more likely than unarmed whites to be killed by police, a result the study called "evidence of a significant bias" (Ross 2015:1). However, other such studies do not find racial bias. In particular, a recent study found that the percentage of African American residents in St. Louis "block groups" (roughly akin to neighborhoods) did not predict the number of police shootings (Klinger et al. 2016).

Individual-Level Research. The research just discussed that yields mixed results uses states, cities, counties, or neighborhoods as its units of analysis. This type of research is called *ecological research.* Other research uses individual police shootings and other uses of force as its units of analysis. This type of research suggests that racial disparities in use of force do reflect racial biases.

For example, in the national survey for the 2002–2011 period discussed earlier for stops and searches, 1.3% of African Americans with police contacts reported experiencing excessive physical force from police, compared to 0.7% of Latinos and 0.5% of non-Latino whites (Hyland et al. 2015). Although these results rely on respondents' perceptions that the force was indeed excessive, they still support the idea that police officers' racial bias influences their use of excessive force.

An analysis of the *Washington Post* data on fatal shootings by police focused on the 93 police shootings in 2015 (out of 990 fatal shootings overall) of unarmed civilians. After adjusting for such factors as whether the civilian was attacking the officer and the crime rate in the neighborhood in which the shooting happened, the analysis found that unarmed African American men were twice as likely to be fatally shot by police than unarmed white men (Nix et al. 2017). The study also found that the unarmed African American men killed by police were less likely than their white counterparts to be attacking police officers or other civilians.

Another example of this research involved a study of 1,846 incidents of police use of nonlethal force against either African American or nonwhite Latino civilians in a large Texan city (Fridell and Lim 2016). The dependent variable for this study was whether an officer had used more severe force (hard empty hand control, pepper spray, or Tasers and other stun guns) versus less severe force (soft empty hand control). Controlling for factors including the suspect's level of resistance and possible weapon possession, the study found that police were more likely to use stun guns against African American suspects than white suspects, but were not more likely to use pepper spray or hard empty hand control. Overall, the study found qualified support for the idea that implicit bias puts African Americans more at risk for police use of force.

A fourth example analyzed use of force data from twelve police departments across the nation (Goff et al. 2016). African Americans were four times more likely than non-Latino whites to experience police use of force, with Latinos slightly less likely than whites to experience such force. Because use of force is more likely during an arrest, the report further determined that African Americans were 28% more likely than whites to experience use of force when being arrested, and that the use of force against arrested African Americans was 32% more severe than against arrested whites. Although these results suggested police bias, the report noted that racial differences might exist in resistance to or disrespect for police, and that any such differences may help account for the racial disparity it found.

A fifth example of individual-level research examined some 6,000 use of force cases in seven U.S. cities (Paoline, Gau, and Terrill 2016). Controlling for the extent of suspect resistance and other factors, this study found that white officers were more likely to use force against African American suspects than against white suspects, while black officers were equally likely to use force against suspects of either race.

Yet another example involved more than 500,000 police stops in New York City (Morrow, White, and Fradella 2017). This study found that the police used force in 14% of these stops, and that they were more likely to do so against African Americans (eight times more likely) and Latinos (five times more likely) than against non-Latino whites. This general difference persisted even when the study controlled for the stopped persons' behavior and other relevant variables.

An interesting variant of this kind of research examined the effects on police use of force after African American suspects fatally shoot police. Focusing on two such shootings in New York City, the study found that use of force against African Americans increased for several days after the shootings occurred, while use of force against Latinos and whites did not increase (Legewie 2016). The study found no effects for two other fatal shootings of police by a Latino and white suspect, respectively.

Interpreting the Evidence

We have seen that evidence of racial bias in police use of force is somewhat inconsistent, with much but not all research finding evidence of such bias. We have also seen that evidence of racial disparity in police use of force is open to several interpretations that do not all equate to actual police bias. Thus, even though many studies find racial disparities in the use of police force, the exact reasons for these disparities remain unclear. Reflecting the complexity of the evidence, a group of researchers recently compiled a comprehensive database of police stops, arrests, and fatal and nonfatal injuries of civilians by police (Miller et al. 2017). They then found that the probability of civilian death or injury from police use of force did not differ by race and ethnicity, leading them to conclude that the ratio of death and injury to stops and arrests is "surprisingly consistent by race and ethnicity" (29).

Additional research is necessary to shed further light on this fundamental issue in race and policing. At this time, it is safe to say that although the research on race and police use of force is not always consistent, substantial evidence does exist of racial bias in use of force. For this reason, police departments need to do everything possible to minimize this bias, as people of color should not have to worry that their race or ethnicity puts their lives and safety in danger when they interact with the police.

SUMMARY

1. Today's criminal justice system has its roots in efforts to control slaves before the Civil War and in efforts to control free blacks after the Civil War. Many commentators say that criminal justice today still aims to control African Americans and other people of color because of these roots and that racism remains entrenched in today's criminal justice.

2. A middle-ground view holds that any racial/ethnic discrimination in today's criminal justice system reflects implicit racial bias and stereotyping that depict people of color, and especially young African American males, as being especially prone to violent crime. Although this discrimination may not be intentional, it is still highly inappropriate and does great harm to individuals of color, their families, and their communities.

3. Perceptions of police racial/ethnic bias and discrimination contribute to negative views about the police among people of color. Their dissatisfaction with police in turn hampers police efforts to control crime.

4. Although the research yields some inconsistent research, police stops and searches often appear to target people of color disproportionately. In particular, people of color tend more often to be searched after being stopped even though they are less likely to possess illegal contraband at the time of their stop.

5. Police appear to arrest people of color out of proportion to their actual involvement in crime. This type of bias may be more likely when victims are whites and when the offenses are misdemeanors.

6. People of color are more likely to experience police use of force, fatal or nonfatal. Simulation research suggests that police racial bias helps account for this problem. Research on this issue tends to support this possibility but also yields some inconsistent results.

KEY TERMS

focal concerns perspective. The view that racial discrimination in criminal justice stems from implicit biases and racial stereotypes in American society that assume people of color, and particularly young African American males, are prone to violent crime

Jim Crow racism. The belief in, and practice of, virulent racist views in the South and elsewhere before the successes of the 1960s civil rights movement

racial profiling. The assumption that someone's race indicates greater potential for criminal behavior

REFERENCES

Alexander, Michelle. 2012. *The New Jim Crow: Mass Incarceration in the Age of Colorblindness*. New York: New Press.

Apuzzo, Matt. 2015. "Ferguson Police Routinely Violate Rights of Blacks, Justice Dept. Finds." *New York Times* March 4:A1.

Baker, Al, J. David Goodman and Benjamin Muellerjune. 2015. "Beyond the Chokehold: The Path to Eric Garner's Death." *The New York Times* June 14:A1.

Berman, Mark. 2017. "Minn. Officer Acquitted in Shooting of Philando Castile during Traffic Stop, Dismissed from Police Force." *Washington Post* June 17. https://www.washingtonpost.com/news/post-nation/wp/2017/06/16/minn-officer-acquitted-of-manslaughter-for-shooting-philando-castile-during-traffic-stop/?utm_term=.67318719e36b

Black, Donald. 1980. "The Social Organization of Arrest." In *Police Behavior: A Sociological Perspective*, edited by Richard J. Lundman, 151–62. New York: Oxford University Press.

Blinder, Alan. 2017. "Ex-Officer Who Shot Walter Scott Pleads Guilty in Charleston." *New York Times* May 3:A10.

Blow, Charles M. 2012. "The Curious Case of Trayvon Martin." *New York Times* March 17:A21.

Branigan, Amelia R., Christopher Wildeman, Jeremy Freese, and Catarina I. Kiefe. 2017. "Complicating Colorism: Race, Skin Color, and the Likelihood of Arrest." *Socius* 3. https://doi.org/10.1177/2378023117725611

Browne-Marshall, Gloria. 2013. *Race, Law, and American Society: 1607 to Present*. New York: Routledge.

Brunson, Rod K. 2007. "'Police Don't Like Black People': African-American Young Men's Accumulated Police Experiences." *Criminology & Public Policy* 6:71–102.

Butler, Paul. 2017. *Chokehold: Policing Black Men.* New York: New Press.

Cannon, Lou. 1998. *Official Negligence: How Rodney King and the Riots Changed Los Angeles and the LAPD.* New York: Times Books.

Correll, Joshua, Bernadette Park, Charles M. Judd, Bernd Wittenbrink, Melody S. Sadler, and Tracie Keesee. 2007. "Across the Thin Blue Line: Police Officers and Racial Bias in the Decision to Shoot." *Journal of Personality and Social Psychology* 92(6):1006–23.

Davis, Angela J. 2017. "Introduction." In *Policing the Black Man: Arrest, Prosecution, and Imprisonment*, edited by Angela J. Davis, xi–xxiv. New York: Pantheon Books.

Davis, Mark. 2017. "Study: Vermont Police Stop, Search Black Drivers More than Whites." *Seven Days* January 9. https://www.sevendaysvt.com/OffMessage/archives/2017/01/09/study-vermont-police-stop-search-black-drivers-more-than-whites

Dempsey, John S., and Linda S. Forst. 2016. *An Introduction to Policing.* Belmont, CA: Cengage Learning.

Eaton, Kristi, and Jaweed Kaleem. 2016. "Anger Grows in Tulsa as Police Release Video of Fatal Shooting of Unarmed Black Man." *Los Angeles Times* September 20. http://www.latimes.com/nation/la-na-terence-crutcher-20160920-snap-story.html

Eckholm, Erik, and Matt Apuzzo. 2015. "Darren Wilson Is Cleared of Rights Violations in Ferguson Shooting." *New York Times* March 5:A1.

Fairfax, Robert A., Jr. 2017. "The Grand Jury and Police Violence against Black Men." In *Policing the Black Man: Arrest, Prosecution, and Imprisonment*, edited by Angela J. Davis, 209–33. New York: Pantheon Books.

Fenton, Justin. 2017. "Five Baltimore Officers from Freddie Gray Case Face Internal Discipline; Three Could Be Fired." *Baltimore Sun* May 22. http://www.baltimoresun.com/news/maryland/freddie-gray/bs-md-ci-freddie-gray-internal-charges-20170522-story.html

Fridell, Lorie, and Hyeyoung Lim. 2016. "Assessing the Racial Aspects of Police Force Using the Implicit- and Counter-Bias Perspectives." *Journal of Criminal Justice* 44:36–48.

Gau, Jacinta M., and Kareem L. Jordan. 2015. "Profiling Trayvon: Young Black Males, Suspicion, and Surveillance." In *Deadly Injustice: Trayvon Martin, Race, and the Criminal Justice System*, edited by Devon Johnson, Patricia Y. Warren, and Amy Farrell, 7–22. New York: New York University Press.

Glaser, Jack. 2015. *Suspect Race: Causes and Consequences of Racial Profiling.* New York: Oxford University Press.

Goff, Phillip Atiba, Tracey Lloyd, Amanda Geller, Steven Raphael, and Jack Glaser. 2016. *The Science of Justice: Race, Arrests, and Police Use of Force.* New York: Center for Policing Equity, John Jay College of Criminal Justice.

Goldstein, Joseph. 2013. "Judge Rejects New York's Stop-and-Frisk Policy." *New York Times* August 13:A1.

Hagan, John, and Marjorie S. Zatz. 1985. "The Social Organization of Criminal Justice Processing Activities." *Social Science Research* 14:103–25.

Harris, David A. 2015. "The Dangers of Racialized Perceptions and Thinking by Law Enforcement." In *Deadly Injustice: Trayvon Martin, Race, and the Criminal Justice System*, edited by Devon Johnson, Patricia Y. Warren, and Amy Farrell, 146–64. New York: New York University Press.

Henning, Kristin. 2017. "Boys to Men: The Role of Policing in the Socialization of Black Boys." In *Policing the Black Man: Arrest, Prosecution, and Imprisonment*, edited by Angela J. Davis, 57–94. New York: Pantheon Books.

Hermann, Peter, Lynh Bui, and Matt Zapotosky. 2016. "Federal Probe Finds Baltimore Police Dept. Racially Discriminated in Practices that Target Blacks." *Washington Post* August 9. https://www.washingtonpost.com/local/public-safety/federal-probe-finds-baltimore-police-dept-racially-discriminated-in-practices-that-target-blacks/2016/08/09/51216804–5e8a-11e6-af8e-54aa2e849447_story.html?utm_term=.09527f7f559c

Hutchins, Renée McDonald. 2017. "Racial Profiling: The Law, the Policy, and the Practice." In *Policing the Black Man: Arrest, Prosecution, and Punishment*, edited by Angela J. Davis, 95–134. New York: Pantheon Books.

Hyland, Shelley, Lynn Langton, and Elizabeth Davis. 2015. *Police Use of Nonfatal Force, 2002–11*. Washington, DC: Bureau of Justice Statistics, U.S. Department of Justice.

Jacobs, David, and David W. Britt. 1979. "Inequality and Police Use of Deadly Force: An Empirical Assessment of the Conflict Hypothesis." *Social Problems* 26:403–12.

Jacobs, David, and Robert M. O'Brien. 1998. "The Determinants of Deadly Force: A Structural Analysis of Police Violence." *American Journal of Sociology* 103:837–62.

James, Lois, Stephen M. James, and Bryan J. Vila. 2016. "The Reverse Racism Effect." *Criminology & Public Policy* 15(2):457–79.

Kelly, Kimbriell, Wesley Lowery, Steven Rich, Julie Tate, and Jennifer Jenkins. 2016. "Fatal Shootings by Police Remain Relatively Unchanged after Two Years." *Washington Post* December 30. https://www.washingtonpost.com/investigations/fatal-shootings-by-police-remain-relatively-unchanged-after-two-years/2016/12/30/fc807596-c3ca-11e6–9578–0054287507db_story.html

Kerner Commission. 1968. *Report of the National Advisory Commission on Civil Disorders*. New York: Bantam Books.

Klinger, David, Richard Rosenfeld, Daniel Isom, and Michael Deckard. 2016. "Race, Crime, and the Micro-Ecology of Deadly Force." *Criminology & Public Policy* 15(1):193–222.

Klinger, David A., and Lee Ann Slocum. 2017. "Critical Assessment of an Analysis of a Journalistic Compendium of Citizens Killed by Police Gunfire." *Criminology & Public Policy* 16(1):349–62.

Kochel, Tammy Rinehart, David B. Wilson, and Stephen D. Mastrofski. 2011. "Effect of Suspect Race on Officers' Arrest Decisions." *Criminology* 49(2):473–512.

LaFraniere, Sharon, and Andrew W. Lehren. 2015. "The Disproportionate Risk of Driving while Black." *New York Times* October 25:A1.

Landler, Mark, and Michael D. Shear. 2013. "President Offers a Personal Take on Race in U.S." *New York Times* July 20:A1.

LeCount, Ryan Jerome. 2017. "More Black than Blue? Comparing the Racial Attitudes of Police to Citizens." *Sociological Forum* 32:1051–72.

Legewie, Joscha. 2016. "Racial Profiling and Use of Force in Police Stops: How Local Events Trigger Periods of Increased Discrimination." *American Journal of Sociology* 122(2):379–424.

Levinson, Justin D., and Robert J. Smith. 2012. *Implicit Racial Bias across the Law.* Cambridge: Cambridge University Press.

Lowery, Wesley. 2016. "Aren't More White People than Black People Killed by Police? Yes, but No." *Washington Post* July 11. https://www.washingtonpost .com/news/post-nation/wp/2016/07/11/arent-more-white-people-than-black-people-killed-by-police-yes-but-no/?utm_term=.9bc3df0d3f48

Lundman, Richard J., and Brian R. Kowalski. 2009. "Speeding while Black? Assessing the Generalizability of Lange et al.'s (2001, 2005) New Jersey Turnpike Speeding Survey Findings." *JQ: Justice Quarterly* 26(3):504–27.

Mann, Coramae Richey. 1993. *Unequal Justice: A Question of Color.* Bloomington: Indiana University Press.

McDonell-Parry, Amelia, and Justine Barron. 2017. "Death of Freddie Gray: 5 Things You Didn't Know." *Rolling Stone* April 12. https://www.rollingstone. com/culture/features/death-of-freddie-gray-5-things-you-didnt-know-w476107

Miller, Ted R., Bruce A. Lawrence, Nancy N. Carlson, Delia Hendrie, Sean Randall, Ian R. H. Rockett, and Rebecca S. Spicer. 2017. "Perils of Police Action: A Cautionary Tale from US Data Sets." *Injury Prevention* 23:27–32.

Morrow, Weston J., Michael D. White, and Henry F. Fradella. 2017. "After the Stop: Exploring the Racial/Ethnic Disparities in Police Use of Force during Terry Stops." *Police Quarterly* 20:367–96.

Muhammad, Khalil Gibran. 2011. *The Condemnation of Blackness: Race, Crime, and the Making of Modern Urban America.* Cambridge, MA: Harvard University Press.

Myrdal, Gunnar. 1944. *An American Dilemma: The Negro Problem and Modern Democracy.* New York: Harper & Brothers.

Nix, Justin, Bradley A. Campbell, Edward H. Byers, and Geoffrey P. Alpert. 2017. "A Bird's Eye View of Civilians Killed by Police in 2015." *Criminology & Public Policy* 16(1):309–40.

Paoline, Eugene A., III, Jacinta M. Gau, and William Terrill. 2016. "Race and the Police Use of Force Encounter in the United States." *British Journal of Criminology.* https://doi.org/10.1093/bjc/azw089

Petersilia, Joan. 1983. *Racial Disparities in the Criminal Justice System*. Santa Monica, CA: Rand.

Plant, E. Ashby, and B. Michelle Peruche. 2005. "The Consequences of Race for Police Officers' Responses to Criminal Suspects." *Psychological Science* 16(3):180–83.

Rector, Kevin. 2016. "Black Motorists in Md. Are Pulled Over, Searched at Higher Rates." *Baltimore Sun* November 16. http://www.baltimoresun.com/news/maryland/crime/bs-md-police-traffic-stops-20161116-story.html

Reisig, Michael D., John D. McCluskey, Stephen D. Mastrofski, and William Terrill. 2004. "Suspect Disrespect toward the Police." *Justice Quarterly* 21:241–68.

Riksheim, Eric, and Steven M. Chermak. 1993. "Causes of Police Behavior Revisited." *Journal of Criminal Justice* 21:353–82.

Rios, Victor M. 2015. "Policed, Punished, Dehumanized: The Reality for Young Men of Color Living in America." In *Deadly Injustice: Trayvon Martin, Race, and the Criminal Justice System*, edited by Devon Johnson, Patricia Y. Warren, and Amy Farrell, 59–80. New York: New York University Press.

Robles, Frances and Jose Del Real. 2018. "8 Bullets Struck Sacramento Man as He Faced Away." *The New York Times* March 31:A1.

Rosenfeld, Richard, Robert Fornango, and Andres F. Rengifo. 2007. "The Impact of Order-Maintenance Policing on New York City Homicide and Robbery Rates: 1988–2001." *Criminology* 45(2):355–84.

Rosich, Katherine J. 2007. *Race, Ethnicity, and the Criminal Justice System*. Washington, DC: American Sociological Association.

Ross, Cody T. 2015. "A Multi-Level Bayesian Analysis of Racial Bias in Police Shootings at the County-Level in the United States, 2011–2014." *PLOS One* 10(11): e0141854. doi:10.1371/journal.pone.54

Russell-Brown, Katheryn. 2009. *The Color of Crime: Racial Hoaxes, White Fear, Black Protectionism, Police Harassment, and Other Macroaggressions*. New York: New York University Press.

———. 2015. "Go Ahead and Shoot—the Law Might Have Your Back: History, Race, Implicit Bias, and Justice in Florida's Stand Your Ground Law." In *Deadly Injustice: Trayvon Martin, Race, and the Criminal Justice System*, edited by Devon Johnson, Patricia Y. Warren, and Amy Farrell, 115–45. New York: New York University Press.

———. 2017. "Making Implicit Bias Explicit." In *Policing the Black Man: Arrest, Prosecution, and Imprisonment*, edited by Angela J. Davis, 135–60. New York: Pantheon Books.

Sadler, Melody S., Joshua Correll, Bernadette Park, and Charles M. Judd. 2012. "The World Is Not Black and White: Racial Bias in the Decision to Shoot in a Multiethnic Context." *Journal of Social Issues* 68(2):286–313.

Skogan, Wesley G., and Kathleen Frydl, eds. 2004. *Fairness and Effectiveness in Policing: The Evidence*. Washington, DC: National Research Council.

Smith, Douglas A., Christy Visher, and Laura A. Davidson. 1984. "Equity and Discretionary Justice: The Influence of Race on Police Arrest Decisions." *Journal of Criminal Law and Criminology* 75:234–49.

Smith, Mitch, Yamiche Alcindor, and Jack Healy. 2017. "Grim Echoes for Families: An Officer Shoots and a Jury Acquits." *New York Times* June 18:A14.

Soffen, Kim. 2016. "The Big Question about Why Police Pull Over So Many Black Drivers." *Washington Post* July 8. https://www.washingtonpost.com/news/wonk/wp/2016/07/08/the-big-question-about-why-police-pull-over-so-many-black-drivers/?utm_term=.37f595a98f9

Spohn, Cassia. 2011. "Race, Ethnicity, and Crime." In *The Oxford Handbook of Crime and Criminal Justice*, edited by Michael Tonry, 321–47. New York: Oxford University Press.

———. 2015. "Race, Crime, and Punishment in the Twentieth and Twenty-First Centuries." *Crime and Justice* 44(1):49–97.

Steffensmeier, Darrell, Noah Painter-Davis, and Jeffery Ulmer. 2017. "Intersectionality of Race, Ethnicity, Gender, and Age on Criminal Punishment." *Sociological Perspectives* 60(4):810–33.

Stevenson, Bryan. 2017. "A Presumption of Guilt: The Legacy of America's History of Racial Injustice." Pp. 3-30 in *Policing the Black Man: Arrest, Prosecution, and Imprisonment*, edited by A. J. Davis. New York: Pantheon Books.

Stewart, Eric A. 2007. "Either They Don't Know or They Don't Care: Black Males and Negative Police Experiences." *Criminology & Public Policy* 6:123–30.

Takagi, Paul. 1974. "A Garrison State in a 'Democratic' Society." *Crime and Social Justice* 1:27–33.

Tillyer, Rob. 2014. "Opening the Black Box of Officer Decision-Making: An Examination of Race, Criminal History, and Discretionary Searches." *Justice Quarterly* 31(6):961–85.

Tillyer, Rob, and Robin S. Engel. 2012. "Racial Differences in Speeding Patterns: Exploring the Differential Offending Hypothesis." *Journal of Criminal Justice* 40(4):285–95.

Walinchus, Lucia, and Richard Pérez-Peña. 2017. "Tulsa Officer Is Acquitted in Killing of Black Driver." *New York Times* May 18:A22.

Weitzer, Ronald, Steven A. Tuch, and Wesley G. Skogan. 2008. "Police-Community Relations in a Majority-Black City." *Journal of Research in Crime and Delinquency* 45(4):398–428.

Wilbanks, William. 1987. *The Myth of a Racist Criminal Justice System*. Monterey, CA: Brooks/Cole.

[6]

RACE, PROSECUTION, AND PUNISHMENT

Chapter Outline

Learning Questions

1. What do comparisons of the racial/ethnic percentages of arrestees and prisoners reveal?
2. How does the victim's race in some research appear to affect charging decisions by prosecutors?
3. What does research on skin tone and sentencing reveal?

4. What is meant by cumulative disadvantage in the criminal justice system?

5. How has the war on drugs discriminated against African Americans and Latinos?

After a person is arrested, a series of decisions ordinarily occurs. The most important decisions belong to the prosecutor, who decides whether to bring charges against a suspect and, if so, which charges to bring; the prosecutor also decides whether to ask a judge to detain a defendant before trial. A judge then decides whether to detain the defendant or, instead, to allow the defendant to be free on bail before trial and, if so, how much bail to require. If there is a trial, a judge or jury decides whether to convict the defendant. If the defendant pleads guilty or is found guilty after a trial, the judge must then decide whether to incarcerate the defendant and, if so, how long the term of incarceration should be. All of these decisions involve much discretion on the part of criminal courts' many participants. As with policing, this discretion opens the door for racial and ethnic bias to occur. What role, if any, do race and ethnicity play in all of these decisions after arrest?

Before proceeding to the research evidence on this role, it is worth discussing some numbers that speak to the possibility of racial discrimination after arrest. These numbers involve the percentages of arrestees and state prison inmates who are African American or Latino. Many factors, of course, affect whether a convicted defendant is sentenced to prison and for how long. The nature of the crime certainly matters, and so do the defendant's prior criminal record and the extent of harm done to a victim. Judges also take into account the defendant's age and other personal information. Still, evidence of possible racial/ethnic discrimination in imprisonment would emerge if African Americans or Latinos were overrepresented among prison inmates compared to their share of arrests (Blumstein 1982; Tonry 2012). Comparisons of the racial/ethnic makeup of arrestees and prisoners thus provide an initial impression of possible discrimination in imprisonment.

Criminologists have performed these comparisons, which show that the percentages of prisoners who are African American or Latino are often somewhat higher than the percentages of arrestees who are from these two groups (Beck and Blumstein 2017; Harris et al. 2009). These differences tend to be greater for minor offenses, for which criminal justice professionals exercise much discretion, than for serious offenses, for which criminal justice professionals usually take a very hard line.

These comparisons yield two conclusions. First, the heavier involvement of African Americans and perhaps Latinos in violent crime accounts for most of their overrepresentation in prison compared to their shares of the national population (Beck and Blumstein 2017; Harris et al. 2009). Second, African American and Latino overrepresentation as prisoners compared to their share of arrests suggests racial discrimination in the criminal justice system, but it does not prove such discrimination. It may stem, for example, from the inability of people of color to obtain effective defense counsel, or from the fact that they have more extensive prior criminal records, especially for minor offenses in view of policing's focus on high-crime urban neighborhoods (Beck and Blumstein 2017). Because these comparisons are thus not the final word on racial discrimination in criminal justice, it is important to consider research of social scientists on actual racial discrimination after arrest. We now turn to this research.

RACE AND PROSECUTION

Prosecutors play a fundamental role in the processing of criminal cases after arrest. As law professor Angela J. Davis (2017:178–179) notes, "Through their charging and plea bargaining powers, prosecutors control the criminal justice system and frequently predetermine the outcome of criminal cases. . . . The consequences can be life-changing for everyone involved— criminal defendants, crime victims, and the families of both."

Despite this importance, research on race and prosecutorial decision-making is fairly limited. The research that does exist explores prosecutors' decisions regarding: (1) whether to have pretrial defendants detained in jail (many defendants cannot afford bail) instead of releasing them on own their own recognizance; (2) whether to drop all charges against a defendant; (3) whether to bring more serious or less serious charges against defendants whose cases are not dropped; and (4) whether to settle on more or less serious charges during plea bargaining (which characterizes most criminal cases). This research typically takes into account the defendant's prior record, the nature of the alleged crime, and other relevant variables.

The evidence from this research is somewhat inconsistent. For example, some research finds that prosecutors are more likely to drop or reduce charges against white defendants than against African American or Latino defendants (Berdejó 2018; Hartley, Maddan, and Spohn 2007); other research finds this racial disadvantage only for young African American males but not for other people of color (Wooldredge 2012); still other research find no racial differences in this charging decision (Shermer and Johnson 2010); and some research even finds that defendants of color are advantaged in this regard (Wooldredge and Thistlethwaite 2004).

This inconsistency partly reflects the fact that different studies examine different crimes in different jurisdictions; what might be true for one type of crime in a specific jurisdiction might not be true for other types of crimes or other jurisdictions (Kutateladze et al. 2014). Even so, a majority of recent charging studies do find apparent racial discrimination in the charging process (Kutateladze, Andiloro, and Johnson 2016), and some research finds that African Americans and Latinos are more likely than non-Latino whites to suffer pretrial detention (Demuth and Steffensmeier 2004; Sutton 2013). Looking at the prosecutorial research overall, a recent review concluded that "minority defendants may be at a disadvantage when it comes to prosecutorial decision-making in criminal cases" (Kutateladze et al. 2016:404).

Some research finds that the race of the victim affects what charges a prosecutor will bring (Myers 2000). In particular, prosecutors tend to bring more serious charges in homicide and rape cases with white victims than with African American victims, and the charges in cases with white victims tend to more severe when the defendant is African American than when the defendant is white. These related findings "raise the disturbing possibility that some prosecutors define the victimization of whites, especially when African Americans are perpetrators, as more serious criminal events than the comparable victimization of African Americans" (Myers 2000:451).

RACE AND CONVICTION

Once prosecution begins, are people of color more likely than whites to be convicted? Chapter 5's discussion of implicit bias and focal concerns suggests that the answer to this question might be yes. Despite this possibility, research on this issue is sparse, partly because most criminal cases are resolved via plea bargaining. Because criminal trials are so scarce, so are judges' and juries' verdicts after trials, yielding little opportunity for researchers to study their verdicts. Much more research thus focuses on sentencing (discussed later in this chapter) than on conviction.

Much of the conviction research that does exist concerns conviction regardless of whether it stems from plea bargaining or a trial. This research yields inconsistent results. Some studies finds that African American and white defendants are equally likely to be convicted in general, but that African Americans are more likely than whites arrested for the same crime to be convicted of a felony rather than a misdemeanor (Spohn 2000). However, other research finds that defendants' race does not affect their chances of a felony conviction (Eisenstein and Jacob 1977; Petersilia 1985). In line with this latter research, a recent study of 703 homicide cases in Chicago found that the race/ethnicity of defendants or victims (African Americans and Latinos versus whites) did not affect the chances of conviction of felony murder (Martin 2013).

Jury Verdicts

Some conviction research focuses specifically on race and jury verdicts. This research involves either real-life jury cases or, more often, mock *juries*, in which participants read about a trial or watch an acted-out trial in person or on video and then decide on a verdict. Again yielding inconsistent results, some studies find that white jurors are more likely to convict African American defendants, while other studies do not find this bias (Williams and Burek 2008). In general, this research finds that defendants' race and ethnicity have only a small impact on jury verdicts, and some research finds no such bias (Farrell et al. 2015).

Three specific jury findings are worth noting. First, jurors are somewhat more likely to acquit defendants of their same race and to convict defendants of a different race (Hunt 2015). This *similarity bias* is found more often when the strength of the evidence is moderate, but less often when it is strongly for or against conviction (Devine 2012). Second, racial bias appears more likely to influence conviction for less serious crimes than for more serious crimes, perhaps because the latter are so serious that there is less room for racial bias to enter into juries' and judges' decision making (Martin 2013). Third, all-white juries are more likely than racially mixed juries to convict African American defendants than white defendants (Anwar, Bayer, and Hjalmarsson 2012).

Most jury research on racial bias compares the fates of African American defendants and non-Latino white defendants. However, some research has examined possible jury bias against Latino defendants. This research tends to find bias against these defendants, especially when they come from lower socioeconomic backgrounds (Hunt 2015).

Wrongful Convictions

A final line of research related to conviction involves **wrongful convictions**, which are convictions that later are overturned (and defendants *exonerated*) because of new DNA or other evidence (such as false witness testimony), or because it was found that police and/or prosecutorial misconduct tainted the original criminal case. It is estimated that between 5,000 and 30,000 wrongful felony convictions occur annually, along with many thousands more wrongful misdemeanor convictions (Acker and Zalman 2017). Research on wrongful convictions finds that, compared to all convictions, they disproportionately involve African American defendants, and especially African American defendants and white victims (Free 2017; Olney and Bonn 2015).

For example, although African Americans comprise 38% of state prison inmates sentenced for homicide (Carson and Anderson 2016), they account for 50% of homicide exonerations; although they comprise 23% of state inmates sentenced for sexual assault, they account for 59% of sexual assault exonerations; and although they comprise 33% of state inmates sentenced for drug offenses, they account for 55% of drug offense exonerations (Gross, Possley, and Stephens 2017). Innocent African Americans are thus more likely than innocent whites to be convicted of these crimes. This type of research points to a strong role of racial bias in wrongful convictions.

RACE AND SENTENCING

Judges determine the sentence for convicted defendants, often within limits provided by state and/or federal legislation. Because judges usually can exercise discretion even within these limits, racial bias may influence the sentences they render. A large amount of research examines the extent to which this influence occurs. This research typically takes into account the seriousness of the crime, the defendant's prior record, and other factors. If people of color are then more likely to receive harsher sentences, that would be evidence of racial bias, however unconscious, on the part of judges. What does the research evidence say?

Reviews of this extensive evidence point to some trends (Baumer 2013; Franklin 2017; Spohn 2015). Many studies find that African Americans, Latinos, and Native Americans are somewhat more likely than whites to be sentenced to prison instead of probation or a fine. Fewer studies find that, once sentenced to prison, they then receive longer prison terms than whites: Some studies find this difference, but others do not find it. These forms of sentencing disadvantage are found more often for African Americans than for Latinos, and especially for young African American and Latino males compared to other combinations of race/ethnicity, gender, and age (Steffensmeier, Painter-Davis, and Ulmer 2017; Warren, Chiricos, and Bales 2012). However, some studies find no racial or ethnic differences in sentencing (Harris et al. 2009; Reitler, Sullivan, and Frank 2013).

Overall, this body of research finds racial/ethnic discrimination more often in the decision to incarcerate (the **in/out decision**) than among sentence lengths for defendants who are ordered to prison (Spohn 2011). It also finds discrimination more often against those convicted of less serious crimes than of more serious crimes (Chen 2008). Finally, harsher sentencing is also found more often when crime victims are white than when they are African American, with judges apparently considering crimes involving white victims to be more important than crimes with African American victims. Reflecting a *racial-threat hypothesis* (Blalock 1967), some research also finds harsher sentencing in counties and states with higher proportions of African Americans (Jacobs, Carmichael, and Kent 2005), but other research does not find this tendency (Ulmer 2012).

Skin Tone and Afrocentric Facial Features

One type of sentencing research finds striking evidence of racial bias (Blair, Judd, and Chapleau 2004; Eberhardt et al. 2006; King and Johnson 2016; Viglione, Hannon, and DeFina 2011). This research concerns the *facial appearance* of defendants. African American and Anglo defendants differ in *skin tone*: Some are lighter, and some are darker. These defendants also have different degrees of traditional *Afrocentric facial features* beyond skin tone, which include a broad nose, full lips, and wiry hair.

This body of research finds that skin tone and facial features are strongly associated with harsher sentencing. In particular, African Americans and whites with darker skin tone receive harsher sentencing than those with lighter skin tone. This research also finds that African Americans and whites with more Afrocentric facial features also receive harsher sentencing than those with less Afrocentric features. Depending on the study, the harsher sentencing involves the in/out imprisonment decision, longer prison terms among those sentenced to prison, or the death penalty in capital cases. In effect, defendants are punished for looking "more black" and thus for presumably suggesting greater danger to criminal justice professionals. Interestingly, some of this research finds that this negative effect of skin tone and Afrocentric features is greater for white defendants than for African American defendants (King and Johnson 2016).

RACE AND PAROLE

Once convicted defendants are sentenced to incarceration, the key decision point becomes **parole**. Unless they are sentenced to life (only about

5% of prison inmates serve life terms), inmates in most states become eligible for early release from prison after they have served one-third of their sentence. A parole board decides whether to release an inmate on parole. Are prisoners of color at a disadvantage when it comes to parole decisions? Do they have to wait longer than white prisoners to be paroled?

There is not much research to answer these questions, and the results of this research are again mixed (Huebner and Bynum 2008; Morgan and Smith 2008). In some studies, African American offenders must wait longer in prison until they are paroled, but other studies find that African Americans and whites serve equal time in prison before parole once relevant factors are controlled.

RACE AND CUMULATIVE DISADVANTAGE IN CRIMINAL JUSTICE

The discussion in Chapter 5 and so far in this chapter has covered the extent of racial/ethnic disparity and discrimination at key stages of the criminal justice system. We have seen that substantial disparity in arrest and incarceration often exists, but that evidence of racial/ethnic bias and discrimination once relevant factors are controlled is sometimes inconsistent. Overall, it seems that racial discrimination does exist throughout all criminal justice stages, but that its extent today is generally not large, with some notable exceptions.

That said, race and ethnicity still make a difference in criminal justice outcomes generally, and more of a difference for some outcomes than for other outcomes. As sentencing expert Marc Mauer (2017:42) observes, "While the racial disparities produced by the system have complex origins and are far less likely to appear as outwardly racist as in the days of Jim Crow, they nonetheless are pervasive at each stage of the system." Scholars note that the many disadvantages, large or small, that people of color often do face during the different stages of the criminal justice system accumulate into a significant **cumulative disadvantage** that helps mightily to account for the racial/ethnic disparities in incarceration that Chapter 1 presented (Kutateladze et al. 2014; Spohn 2015; Sutton 2013).

SPECIAL TOPICS: THE WAR ON DRUGS, CAPITAL PUNISHMENT, AND JUVENILE JUSTICE

Although the evidence of racial/ethnic bias and discrimination in criminal justice is sometimes inconsistent, there are two areas in which this evidence is compelling: (1) the legal war on drugs, and (2) capital punishment. Meanwhile, juvenile justice is an area for which there is some evidence of racial/ethnic discrimination. We now turn to these areas.

The War on Drugs

Chapter 1 stated that the legal war on drugs that began in the 1980s has helped account for the serious overrepresentation of African Americans and Latinos in today's prisons. In 2016, African Americans comprised 27% of those arrested for drugs and 31% of state prisoners sentenced for drug offenses (Carson 2018; Federal Bureau of Investigation 2017). They also comprised 38% of federal prisoners sentenced for drug offenses. In 1991, when the war against drugs was in full force, drug offenses accounted for 38.5% of new state prison admissions of African Americans, compared to only 19.3% of new prison admissions of whites (Carson and Golinelli 2013). All of these figures for African Americans are much larger than their 13% share of the national population. Reflecting this huge disparity, and taking into account population size, African Americans have been 4.5 times more likely than whites in recent years to be arrested for drug offenses (Mitchell and Caudy 2015), and during the 1980s were seven times more likely than whites to be arrested for these offenses (Spohn 2015).

This general disparity exists even though African Americans' rate of drug offending (using illegal drugs or selling them) is generally no higher than the rate of non-Latino whites (Alexander 2012; Mitchell and Caudy 2015; Vaughn et al. 2017). This fact means that "the racial disparities in arrest rates for using or possessing drugs and for selling drugs cannot be explained away by racial disparities in rates of drug offending" (Spohn 2015:67). The swelling population of African Americans in the nation's prisons from the war on drugs led law professor Michelle Alexander (2012) to famously call the drug war "the new Jim Crow."

Meanwhile, although Latinos represent only 18% of the population, they comprised 20% of drug arrests in 2016 and 20% of state prisoners sentenced for drug offenses. Meanwhile, their share of federal prisoners sentenced for drug offenses was a very high 38.6% (Carson 2018), even though Latinos are also not more likely than Anglos to commit drug offenses (Mitchell and Caudy 2017). In the early 2000s, more than one-third of all new prison admissions for Latinos were for drug offenses (Carson and Golinelli 2013). If, as we have seen in this and the previous chapter, the effects of race and ethnicity on criminal justice outcomes are sometimes inconsistent and only modest in size, their effects on arrests and prosecutions for drug offenses are stronger and more consistent and amount to what has been called "the racially skewed impact of drug law enforcement and sentencing" (Mauer 2017:39).

Research indicates that the racial/ethnic disparity in arrests and imprisonment for drug offenses reflects several factors (Mitchell and Caudy 2017), including the following:

- racial stereotyping and implicit bias by police (Beckett et al. 2005; Mitchell and Caudy 2015);
- targeting by police of drug sales and use in inner cities as opposed to areas containing more whites (Beckett et al. 2005; Spohn 2015); and
- long mandatory minimum sentences for drug offenses, including stiffer legal penalties for crack cocaine, which people of color tend to use, than for powder cocaine, which whites tend to use, and which is pharmacologically identical to crack (Alexander 2012; Tonry 2012).

The focus on crack cocaine and the severe penalties for its use and sale that began in the 1980s guaranteed that people of color would be disproportionately arrested and prosecuted and more severely punished, and so they were. As Chapter 1 explained, the war on drugs contributed greatly to growing racial disparities in incarceration during the 1980s and 1990s. Research shows that 20% of African American males born between 1965 and 1969 had gone to prison by 1999, compared to only 3% of their white counterparts. For those African American males without a college degree, 30% had been in prison by 1999, and for African American male high school dropouts, 60% had been in prison (Western 2006). This alarming situation makes the statement in Chapter 1 by a notable criminologist worth repeating: "What is particularly troublesome . . . is the degree to which the impact [of the war against drugs] has been so disproportionately imposed on nonwhites. . . . One can be reasonably confident that if a similar assault was affecting the white community, there would be a strong and effective effort to change either the laws or the enforcement policy" (Blumstein 1993:4–5).

The Opioid Crisis

During the past several years, the United States has been facing what is commonly termed an opioid crisis or epidemic: Approximately 50,000 people died in 2016 from opioid overdoses (Centers for Disease Control and Prevention 2017). This problem has mainly affected white Americans: Whites accounted for 90% of opioid deaths in 2015, while African Americans accounted for only 8%, far short of their share of the national population (McKenzie 2017).

News media coverage has treated the opioid crisis and opioid addicts much more sympathetically than it has treated African American and Latino illegal drug use over the years (Shaw 2017). In the same vein, many critics of the drug war observe that politicians have expressed sympathy and voted for billions of dollars in medical and other aid for today's opioid addicts, while people of color who use illegal drugs are instead arrested and prosecuted (Thrasher 2017). Sociology professor and author Michael Eric Dyson has asserted, "White brothers and sisters have been medicalized in terms of their trauma and addiction. Black and brown people have been criminalized for their trauma and addiction" (McKenzie 2017). In short, white opioid offenders have won America's compassion, while African American and Latino drug offenders have suffered America's punishment. As a recent news report observed, "The fact that the opioid epidemic is primarily striking the majority race helps explain why it is largely being called an epidemic and treated as a public health crisis rather than a war" (McKenzie 2017). The more sympathetic reaction to the opioid crisis underscores the view of drug war critics that this has been primarily a war against people of color. In the blunt words of a recent op-ed headline, "The war on drugs is racist" (Thrasher 2017).

Capital Punishment

We saw earlier that research on conviction and sentencing reveals inconsistent findings on the effects of race and ethnicity, and that any effects are usually modest rather than strong. The war on drugs is a notable exception to this general pattern, and so is capital punishment. Research shows that race greatly affects the likelihood of prosecutors deciding to seek the death penalty in capital cases, of defendants being convicted of capital homicide, and of defendants receiving the death penalty if convicted (Bohm 2017).

In this regard, the defendant's race matters in some studies but not all, with African American defendants more likely than white defendants to experience all of these negative outcomes. Overall, the effect of the defendant's race on these outcomes is rather inconsistent and modest. However, the effect of the *victim's* race on these outcomes is stronger and more consistent. Simply put, these outcomes are much more likely when homicide victims are white than when they are African American or Latino, and they are especially likely when the homicide offender is African American and the victim is white (Jennings et al. 2017; Vito, Higgins, and Vito 2014). For example, a California study found that capital cases involving white victims were 3.7 times more likely than those involving African American victims, and 4.7 times more likely than those involving Latino victims, to result in a death penalty sentence (Pierce and Radelet 2005). The evidence regarding the victim's race amounts to what has been called "substantial discrimination in the application of the death penalty" (Spohn 2011:337), and it strongly suggests that criminal justice professionals and juries somehow value the lives of white victims more than the lives of African American victims.

Juvenile Justice

Youths of color are much more likely than Anglo youths to be detained by police, to be referred to juvenile court, and to be sent to residential facilities. Juvenile justice officials and scholars use the term

disproportionate minority contact (DMC) to refer to this overrepresentation of youths of color in the juvenile justice system.

Ample evidence of DMC exists. Although African American and Latino youths comprise only about one-third of all youths, they comprise two-thirds of juvenile offenders in residential placement (correctional confinement) (Office of Juvenile Justice and Delinquency Prevention 2017). African American youths are five times more likely than white youths nationwide to be committed to residential facilities (The Sentencing Project 2017a). In some states, they are at least 10 times more likely than white youths to be sent to residential facilities. Compared to white youths, Latino youths are 1.6 times more likely nationwide to be sent to residential facilities and at least five times more likely in several states (The Sentencing Project 2017b). Meanwhile, Native American youths are three times more likely nationwide to be sent to residential facilities, with this ratio reaching as high as four times in several states (The Sentencing Project 2017c).

As with the adult criminal justice system that this chapter has examined, a key theoretical and practical question for juvenile justice is whether DMC stems primarily from racial/ethnic differences in offending or from racial bias and discrimination in juvenile justice. Racial/ethnic differences in offending (see Chapter 3) do explain some of DMC. However, racial bias and discrimination also matter in many studies (Bishop and Leiber 2012; Peck, Leiber, and Brubaker 2014), as the extent of DMC far exceeds any differences in offending (Rovner 2016). For example, recent studies find that African American and Latino youths are twice as likely as Anglo youths to be sent to correctional confinement even after controlling for the youths' offending risk (Mallett and Stoddard-Dare 2010; Rodriguez 2013). However, some research finds that youths of color are not more likely than white youths to be sent to confinement (Holleran and Stout 2017). Turning to another harsh juvenile justice outcome, being waived (transferred) to criminal court, a recent review concluded that juvenile race in most studies does not directly predict this outcome but may predict it in conjunction with other factors such as age and location (Zane, Welsh, and Drakulich 2016).

Various juvenile justice reforms during the past few decades may have reduced or eliminated DMC, thus accounting for the inconsistent findings in recent DMC research (Peck, Leiber, and Brubaker 2014). However, the extent of this reduction varies by state, and DMC continues in many locations (Leiber, Bishop, and Chamlin 2011). Overall, then, the effect of race and ethnicity on juvenile justice outcomes parallels that of criminal justice system outcomes (Campbell et al. 2017). This effect is often variable, with its existence and size depending on which specific outcome is being examined. However, because many studies find that race and/or ethnicity do matter for juvenile justice outcomes, even if other studies do not find this result, a fair conclusion is that racial/ethnic discrimination does help account for DMC.

A FINAL WORD ON RACE AND DIFFERENTIAL INVOLVEMENT IN CRIMINAL JUSTICE

Chapter 1 posed the question of the extent to which differential racial involvement in the criminal justice system reflects differential racial involvement in crime versus discriminatory practices by criminal justice professionals. Other chapters have presented evidence that racial differences in serious conventional crime do exist (Chapter 3), but that discriminatory practices by criminal justice professionals also occur (Chapter 5 and this chapter). Although evidence of these practices is sometimes inconsistent, it does signal that America's criminal justice system falls far short of treating all people equally regardless of their race and ethnicity, even in the post–Jim Crow era.

Scholars continue to debate which of these two dynamics, differential involvement in crime versus discriminatory practices in criminal justice, contributes more to differential involvement in criminal justice. For now the best conclusion is that both dynamics seem to matter. As criminologist Cassia Spohn (2011:333–334) observes, "It seems reasonable to conclude that the racial disproportionality in the prison population results to a large extent from racial disparities in criminal involvement but to some extent from racial discrimination at various stages in the criminal justice process, including sentencing." She continues, "Persuasive evidence exists that racial minorities . . . are subject to racial profiling, and they are more likely than whites to be shot and killed, arrested, and victimized by excessive physical force. Compelling evidence also points to . . . racial bias in decisions regarding bail, charging, plea bargaining, jury selection, sentencing, and juvenile justice processing" (339). Sentencing expert Marc Mauer (2017:42) agrees: "While the racial disparities produced by the [criminal justice] system have complex origins and are far less likely to appear as outwardly racist as in the days of Jim Crow, they nonetheless are pervasive at each stage of the system." However unintended this pattern of bias and discrimination might usually be, it does great harm to people of color and is simply unacceptable in a nation that aspires to "liberty and justice for all."

SUMMARY

1. Comparisons of the percentages of arrestees and state prison inmates who are African Americans or Latino reveal possible racial/ethnic disparities in incarceration for certain crimes, especially for minor offenses.

2. Although the evidence on race and prosecutorial decision making is inconsistent, the majority of recent studies find apparent discrimination in the charging process. Some research also finds that prosecutors bring more serious charges when victims are white than when they are African American.

3. The evidence on race and conviction is fairly sparse and also inconsistent, but some research does find people of color at a disadvantage. Jurors tend to be more likely to convict defendants of a different race/ethnicity and to acquit defendants of their own race/ethnicity. Wrongful conviction data find that African American defendants are much more likely than white defendants to be wrongfully convicted. As well, conviction of people of color appears more likely when the evidence of guilt is moderate and when the alleged crime is less serious.

4. Much research on race/ethnicity and sentencing yields complex results. Discrimination in sentencing occurs more often for the in/out imprisonment decision than for sentence length. Sentencing disadvantage is found more often and more severely for young African American males than for other combinations of race/ethnicity, age, and gender.

5. Growing research finds that people with darker skin tone and more Afrocentric facial features are more likely to receive harsher sentences.

6. Research on race and parole is sparse and yields inconsistent results, with people of color at a disadvantage in parole decisions in some studies but not in other studies.

7. Racial discrimination in sentencing is especially pronounced in drug cases. African Americans and Latinos are more likely than whites both to be arrested for drug offenses and to be sentenced to prison for drug offenses, even though they are not generally more likely than whites to commit drug offenses. The legal war against drugs has been primarily a war against African Americans and Latinos.

8. Sentencing in capital cases is racially discriminatory. The death penalty is more common in some studies for African American defendants, but the more consistent finding is that the death penalty is more common in capital cases with white victims.

9. The effect of race and ethnicity on juvenile justice outcomes is often variable, with its existence and size depending on which specific outcome is being examined. Many studies do find juveniles' race/ethnicity affecting juvenile justice decisions about them, but other studies do not find this evidence.

KEY TERMS

cumulative disadvantage. In criminal justice, the idea that the many disadvantages people of color often face during the different stages of the criminal justice system accumulate and help explain the large racial/ethnic disparities in mass incarceration

disproportionate minority contact. The overrepresentation of youths of color in the juvenile justice system.

in/out decision. A judge's decision regarding whether to incarcerate a convicted defendant

parole. Early release from prison as determined by a parole board

wrongful convictions. Convictions of defendants who are in fact not guilty

REFERENCES

Acker, James R., and Marvin Zalman. 2017. "Taking Stock of Innocence: Movements, Mountains, and Wrongful Convictions." *Journal of Contemporary Criminal Justice* 33(1):8–25.

Alexander, Michelle. 2012. *The New Jim Crow: Mass Incarceration in the Age of Colorblindness.* New York: New Press.

Anwar, Shamena, Patrick Bayer, and Randi Hjalmarsson. 2012. "The Impact of Jury Race in Criminal Trials." *Quarterly Journal of Economics* 127(2): 1017–55.

Baumer, Eric P. 2013. "Reassessing and Redirecting Research on Race and Sentencing." *Justice Quarterly* 30(2):231–61.

Beck, Allen J., and Alfred Blumstein. 2017. "Racial Disproportionality in U.S. State Prisons: Accounting for the Effects of Racial and Ethnic Differences in Criminal Involvement, Arrests, Sentencing, and Time Served." *Journal of Quantitative Criminology.* DOI 10.1007/s10940-017-9357-6.

Beckett, Katherine, Kris Nyrop, Lori Pfingst, and Melissa Bowen. 2005. "Drug Use, Drug Possession Arrests, and the Question of Race: Lessons from Seattle." *Social Problems* 52:419–41.

Berdejó, Carlos. 2018. "Criminalizing Race: Racial Disparities in Plea Bargaining." *Boston College Law Revierw* 59:forthcoming.

Bishop, Donna M., and Michael J. Leiber. 2012. "Racial and Ethnic Differences in Delinquency and Justice System Responses." In *The Oxford Handbook of Juvenile Crime and Juvenile Justice*, edited by Barry C. Feld and Donna M. Bishop, 445-484. New York: Oxford University Press.

Blair, Irene V., Charles M. Judd, and Kristine M. Chapleau. 2004. "The Influence of Afrocentric Facial Features in Criminal Sentencing." *Psychological Science* 15:674–79.

Blalock, Hubert. 1967. *Toward a Theory of Minority-Group Relations.* New York: John Wiley.

Blumstein, Alfred. 1982. "On the Racial Disproportionality of United States Prison Populations." *Journal of Criminal Law and Criminology* 73:1260–81.

———.1993. "Making Rationality Relevant—The American Society of Criminology 1992 Presidential Address." *Criminology* 31(1):1–16.

Bohm, Robert M. 2017. *Deathquest: An Introduction to the Theory and Practice of Capital Punishment in the United States*. New York: Routledge.

Campbell, Nordia A., Ashlee R. Barnes, Amber Mandalari, Eyitayo Onifade, Christina A. Campbell, Valerie R. Anderson, Deborah A. Kashy, and William S. Davidson. 2017. "Disproportionate Minority Contact in the Juvenile Justice System: An Investigation of Ethnic Disparity in Program Referral at Disposition." *Journal of Ethnicity in Criminal Justice*. https://doi-org.prxy4.ursus.maine.edu/10.1080/15377938.2017.1347544

Carson, E. Ann. 2018. *Prisoners in 2016*. Washington, DC: Bureau of Justice Statistics.

Carson, E. Ann, and Daniela Golinelli. 2013. *Prisoners in 2012: Trends in Admissions and Releases, 1991–2012* Washington, DC: Bureau of Justice Statistics, U.S. Department of Justice.

Centers for Disease Control and Prevention. 2017. "Provisional Counts of Drug Overdose Deaths, as of 8/6/2017." https://www.cdc.gov/nchs/data/health_policy/monthly-drug-overdose-death-estimates.pdf

Chen, Elsa Y. 2008. "The Liberation Hypothesis and Racial and Ethnic Disparities in the Application of California's Three Strikes Law." *Journal of Ethnicity in Criminal Justice* 6(2):83–102.

Davis, Angela J. 2017. "The Prosecution of Black Men." In *Policing the Black Man: Arrest, Prosecution, and Imprisonment*, edited by Angela J. Davis, 178–208. New York: Pantheon Books.

Demuth, Stephen, and Darrell Steffensmeier. 2004. "The Impact of Gender and Race-Ethnicity in the Pretrial Release Process." *Social Problems* 51: 222–42.

Devine, Dennis J. 2012. *Jury Decision Making: The State of the Science*. New York: New York University Press.

Eberhardt, Jennifer L., Paul G. Davies, Valerie J. Purdie-Vaughns, and Sheri Lynn Johnson. 2006. "Looking Deathworthy: Perceived Stereotypicality of Black Defendants Predicts Capital-Sentencing Outcomes." *Psychological Science* 17(5):383–86.

Eisenstein, James, and Hebert Jacob. 1977. *Felony Justice: An Organizational Analysis of Criminal Courts*. Boston: Little, Brown.

Farrell, Amy, Patricia Y. Warren, Devon Johnson, Jordyn L. Rosario, and Daniel Givelber. 2015. "The Acquittal of George Zimmerman: Race and Judges' Perceptions about the Accuracy of Not Guilty Verdicts." In *Deadly Injustice: Trayvon Martin, Race, and the Criminal Justice system*, edited by Devon Johnson, Patricia Y. Warren, and Amy Farrell, 165–84. New York: New York University Press.

Federal Bureau of Investigation. 2017. *Crime in the United States, 2016.* Washington, DC: Federal Bureau of Investigation.

Franklin, Travis W. 2017. "The State of Race and Punishment in America: Is Justice Really Blind?" *Journal of Criminal Justice.*

Free, Marvin D., Jr. 2017. "Wrongful Convictions: the African American Experience." *Sociology of Crime, Law & Deviance* 22:7–25.

Gross, Samuel R., Maurice Possley, and Klara Stephens. 2017. *Race and Wrongful Convictions in the United States.* Irvine: National Registry of Exonerations, University of California, Irvine.

Harris, Casey T., Darrell Steffensmeier, Jeffrey T. Ulmer, and Noah Painter-Davis. 2009. "Are Blacks and Hispanics Disproportionately Incarcerated Relative to Their Arrests? Racial and Ethnic Disproportionality Between Arrest and Incarceration." *Race and Social Problems* 1:187–99.

Hartley, Richard D., Sean Maddan, and Cassia C. Spohn. 2007. "Prosecutorial Discretion: An Examination of Substantial Assistance Departures in Federal Crack-Cocaine and Powder-Cocaine Cases." *JQ: Justice Quarterly* 24(3):382–407.

Holleran, David, and Bruce D. Stout. 2017. "The Importance of Race in Juvenile Commitment in the New Jersey Family Court." *Crime & Delinquency* 63(3):353–72.

Huebner, Beth M., and Timothy S. Bynum. 2008. "The Role of Race and Ethnicity in Parole Decisions." *Criminology* 46(4):907–38.

Hunt, Jennifer S. 2015. "Race, Ethnicity, and Culture in Jury Decision Making." *Annual Review of Law & Social Science* 11:269–88.

Jacobs, David, Jason T. Carmichael, and Stephanie L. Kent. 2005. "Vigilantism, Current Racial Threat, and Death Sentences." *American Sociological Review* 70:656–77.

Jennings, Wesley G., John K. Cochran, Caitlin N. Meade, M. Dwayne Smith, Sondra J. Fogel, and Beth Bjerregaard. 2017. "The Impact of the Rape/Sexual Assault Statutory Aggravating Factor on Death Sentencing Decision Making in Capital Murder Trials in North Carolina (1977–2009): A Propensity Score Matching Approach." *Women & Criminal Justice* 27(3):139–50.

King, Ryan D., and Brian D. Johnson. 2016. "A Punishing Look: Skin Tone and Afrocentric Features in the Halls of Justice." *American Journal of Sociology* 122(1):90–124.

Kutateladze, Besiki L., Nancy R. Andiloro, Brian D. Johnson, and Cassia C. Spohn. 2014. "Cumulative Disadvantage: Examining Racial and Ethnic Disparity in Prosecution and Sentencing." *Criminology* 52(3):514–51.

Kutateladze, Besiki Luka, Nancy R. Andiloro, and Brian D. Johnson. 2016. "Opening Pandora's Box: How Does Defendant Race Influence Plea Bargaining?" *Justice Quarterly* 33(3):398–426.

Leiber, Michael, Donna Bishop, and Mitchell B. Chamlin. 2011. "Juvenile Justice Decision-Making before and after the Implementation of the

Disproportionate Minority Contact (DMC) Mandate." *JQ: Justice Quarterly* 28(3):460–92.

Mallett, Christopher A., and Patricia Stoddard-Dare. 2010. "Predicting Secure Detention Placement for African-American Juvenile Offenders: Addressing the Disproportionate Minority Confinement Problem." *Journal of Ethnicity in Criminal Justice* 8:91–103.

Martin, Christine. 2013. "Conviction Odds in Chicago Homicide Cases: Does Race/Ethnicity Matter?" *Journal of Ethnicity in Criminal Justice* 11(1/2):22–43.

Mauer, Marc. 2017. "The Endurance of Racial Disparity in the Criminal Justice System." In *Policing the Black Man: Arrest, Prosecution, and Imprisonment*, edited by Angela J. Davis, 31–56. New York: Pantheon Books.

McKenzie, Kevin. 2017. "Opioid Crisis Points to Racial Divide." *USA Today* March 27. https://www.usatoday.com/story/news/2017/03/27/opioid-crisis-points-racial-divide/99706092/

Mitchell, Ojmarrh, and Michael S. Caudy. 2015. "Examining Racial Disparities in Drug Arrests." *Justice Quarterly* 32(2):288–313.

———. 2017. "Race Differences in Drug Offending and Drug Distribution Arrests." *Crime & Delinquency* 63(2):91–112.

Morgan, Kathryn D., and Brent Smith. 2008. "The Impact of Race on Parole Decision-Making." *JQ: Justice Quarterly* 25(2):411–35.

Myers, Martha A. 2000. "The Social World of America's Courts." In *Criminology: A Contemporary Handbook*, edited by Joseph F. Sheley, 447–71. Belmont, CA: Wadsworth.

Office of Juvenile Justice and Delinquency Prevention. 2017. "Statistical Briefing Book." https://www.ojjdp.gov/ojstatbb/corrections/qa08205.asp?qaDate=2015&text=yes&maplink=link1

Olney, Maeve, and Scott Bonn. 2015. "An Exploratory Study of the Legal and Non-Legal Factors Associated with Exoneration for Wrongful Conviction: The Power of DNA Evidence." *Criminal Justice Policy Review* 26(4):400–20.

Peck, Jennifer H., Michael J. Leiber, and Sarah Jane Brubaker. 2014. "Gender, Race, and Juvenile Court Outcomes: An Examination of Status Offenders." *Youth Violence & Juvenile Justice* 12(3):250–67.

Pierce, Glenn L. and Michael Radelet. 2005. "The Impact of Legally Inappropriate Factors on Death Sentencing for California Homicides, 1990-1999." *Santa Clara Law Review* 46:1-47.

Petersilia, Joan. 1985. "Racial Disparities in the Criminal Justice System: A Summary." *Crime and Delinquency* 31:15–34.

Reitler, Angela K., Christopher J. Sullivan, and James Frank. 2013. "The Effects of Legal and Extralegal Factors on Detention Decisions in US District Courts." *JQ: Justice Quarterly* 30(2):340–68.

Rodriguez, Nancy. 2013. "Concentrated Disadvantage and the Incarceration of Youth: Examining How Context Affects Juvenile Justice." *Journal of Research in Crime and Delinquency* 50:189–215.

Rovner, Joshua. 2016. *Racial Disparities in Youth Commitments and Arrests*. Washington, DC: The Sentencing Project.

Sentencing Project, The. 2017a. "Fact Sheet: Black Disparities in Youth Incarceration." http://www.sentencingproject.org/wp-content/uploads/2017/09/Black-Disparities-in-Youth-Incarceration.pdf

———. 2017b. "Fact Sheet: Latino Disparities in Youth Incarceration." http://www.sentencingproject.org/wp-content/uploads/2017/10/Latino-Disparities-in-Youth-Incarceration.pdf

———. 2017c. "Fact Sheet: Native Disparities in Youth Incarceration." http://www.sentencingproject.org/wp-content/uploads/2017/10/Native-Disparities-in-Youth-Incarceration.pdf

Shaw, Michael. 2017. "Photos Reveal Media's Softer Tone on Opioid Crisis." *Columbia Journalism Review* July 26. https://www.cjr.org/criticism/opioid-crisis-photos.php

Shermer, Lauren O'Neill, and Brian D. Johnson. 2010. "Criminal Prosecutions: Examining Prosecutorial Discretion and Charge Reductions in U.S. Federal District Courts." *JQ: Justice Quarterly* 27(3):394–430.

Spohn, Cassia. 2011. "Race, Ethnicity, and Crime." In *The Oxford Handbook of Crime and Criminal Justice*, edited by Michael Tonry, 321–47. New York: Oxford University Press.

———. 2015. "Race, Crime, and Punishment in the Twentieth and Twenty-First Centuries." *Crime and Justice* 44(1):49–97.

Spohn, Cassia C. 2000. "Thirty Years of Sentencing Reform: The Quest for a Racially Neutral Sentencing Process." In *Policies, Processes, and Decisions of the Criminal Justice System*, edited by Julie Horney, 427–501. Washington, DC: National Institute of Justice.

Steffensmeier, Darrell, Noah Painter-Davis, and Jeffery Ulmer. 2017. "Intersectionality of Race, Ethnicity, Gender, and Age on Criminal Punishment." *Sociological Perspectives* 60(4):810–33.

Sutton, John R. 2013. "Structural Bias in the Sentencing of Felony Defendants." *Social Science Research* 42(5):1207–21.

Thrasher, Steven W. 2017. "The War on Drugs Is Racist. Donald Trump Is Embracing It with Open Arms." *Guardian* April 17. https://www.theguardian.com/commentisfree/2017/apr/17/war-drugs-racist-donald-trump-embracing-open-arms

Tonry, Michael. 2012. *Punishing Race: A Continuing American Dilemma*. New York: Oxford University Press.

Ulmer, Jeffrey T. 2012. "Recent Developments and New Directions in Sentencing Research." *Justice Quarterly* 29:1–40.

Vaughn, Michael G., Christopher P. Salas-Wright, David Cordova, Erik J. Nelson, and Lisa Jaegers. 2017. "Racial and Ethnic Trends in Illicit Drug Use and Binge Drinking among Adolescent and Young Adult Offenders in the United States." *Journal of Criminal Justice*.

Viglione, Jill, Lance Hannon, and Robert DeFina. 2011. "The Impact of Light Skin on Prison Time for Black Female Offenders: A Research Note." *Social Science Journal* 48:250–58.

Vito, Gennaro, George Higgins, and Anthony Vito. 2014. "Capital Sentencing in Kentucky, 2000–2010." *American Journal of Criminal Justice* 39(4):753–70.

Warren, Patricia, Ted Chiricos, and William Bales. 2012. "The Imprisonment Penalty for Young Black and Hispanic Males: A Crime-Specific Analysis." *Journal of Research in Crime & Delinquency* 49(1):56–80.

Western, Bruce. 2006. *Punishment and Inequality in America.* New York: Russell Sage Foundation.

Williams, Marian R., and Melissa W. Burek. 2008. "Justice, Juries, and Convictions: The Relevance of Race in Jury Verdicts." *Journal of Crime & Justice* 31(1):149–69.

Wooldredge, John. 2012. "Distinguishing Race Effects on Pre-trial Release and Sentencing Decisions." *JQ: Justice Quarterly* 29(1):41–75.

Wooldredge, John, and Amy Thistlethwaite. 2004. "Bilevel Disparities in Court Dispositions for Intimate Assault." *Criminology* 42:417–56.

Zane, Steven N., Brandon C. Welsh, and Kevin M. Drakulich. 2016. "Assessing the Impact of Race on the Juvenile Waiver Decision: A Systematic Review and Meta-analysis." *Journal of Criminal Justice* 46:106–17.

[7]

EPILOGUE: WHERE DO WE GO FROM HERE? THE FUTURE OF RACE, CRIME, AND JUSTICE IN THE UNITED STATES

Chapter Outline

What Have You Learned from This Book?
What the Nation Can Do
    Addressing the Causes of Crime
    Reforming Criminal Justice
What You Can Do

Learning Questions

1. What were some key points regarding racial disparities in criminal behavior discussed in this book?
2. What were some key points regarding racial disparities in crime victimization discussed in this book?
3. How would community crime prevention help reduce racial disparities in crime and victimization?
4. How would criminal justice reforms help reduce racial disparities in criminal justice involvement?
5. What can ordinary citizens do to help reduce racial disparities in crime and justice?

The title of this chapter borrows from Dr. Martin Luther King, Jr.'s (1968) last book, *Where Do We Go from Here: Chaos or Community?*, in which he called for continued nonviolent social activism to achieve racial and economic equality. This final chapter summarizes what readers will have learned from the earlier chapters and proposes some measures to reduce both the disproportionate involvement of people of color in criminal behavior and their disproportionate involvement in the criminal justice system. Befitting Dr. King's book, this chapter's proposals include social policies to reduce poverty and racial inequality in our society, and measures to reduce racial discrimination in the criminal justice system. In the spirit of Dr. King, the chapter's final section encourages readers to become social activists to reduce the continuing American dilemma of race, crime, and justice.

WHAT HAVE YOU LEARNED FROM THIS BOOK?

This book examined various aspects of race/ethnicity, crime, and justice in America. A summary of each chapter will illustrate what readers will have learned about these important aspects.

Chapter 1's introductory discussion reminded readers of the extent of racial prejudice and inequality in the United States. It also reviewed the rise of mass incarceration, showing how severely this policy has affected people of color. Although African Americans and Latinos together comprise about 31% of the American population, they account for about 55% of all state prisoners and 69% of all federal prisoners. Scholars continue to debate the extent to which this overrepresentation stems from more frequent criminal behavior by people of color versus racial/ethnic bias and discrimination within the criminal justice system. The chapter emphasized that almost all people of color do not commit conventional crime and that the corporate executives and professionals who commit white-collar crime are almost always white.

Chapter 2's focus on news media and public opinion highlighted several forms of racial/ethnic bias in news media coverage of crime, and it examined racial differences in public opinion about crime and justice. Crime stories in newspapers and on television tend to overrepresent African Americans and Latinos as suspects and also to overrepresent whites as victims. Some stories also feature African Americans and Latino suspects in more menacing contexts. This type of coverage may contribute to white Americans' perceptions of African Americans and Latinos as criminals, raise their fear of crime, and increase their support for harsher punishment of criminals. Relatedly, racial prejudice among whites increases their support for capital punishment and other harsh legal punishment. In other racial differences, people of color hold much more negative views about the police and are much more likely to perceive injustice in the criminal justice system.

Chapter 3 examined the essential issue of racial differences in criminal behavior and the reasons for these differences. Arrest, victimization, and self-report data all indicate that African Americans and Latinos indeed disproportionately commit violent and property crime. Most criminologists attribute this involvement to the poverty and other negative conditions in which people of color live, the everyday racial mistreatment they experience, and cultural codes favoring violent responses to perceived slights and insults. This chapter also noted that certain protective factors help keep African American youths' crime rates lower than might be expected from their life circumstances, and reminded readers that whites commit almost all the white-collar crime that is more damaging than conventional crime.

Chapter 4 examined racial/ethnic differences in crime victimization. Victimization rates are higher for African Americans, Latinos, and Native Americans than for non-Latino whites. This difference reflects these groups' greater likelihood of living in disadvantaged locations conducive to victimization, as well as their higher offending rates. Although many whites fear victimization by African Americans, crime victimization of whites tends to be very intraracial; for Native Americans it tends to be interracial.

Chapters 5 and 6 examined possible racial/ethnic bias and discrimination in the criminal justice system, with Chapter 5 focusing on policing. In that chapter we saw that today's criminal justice system originated in efforts to control slaves before the Civil War and in efforts to control free blacks after the Civil War, with many commentators saying that criminal justice still exists to control African Americans. The chapter argued that racial/ethnic discrimination in criminal justice today reflects implicit racial bias and ste-reotyping that depict people of color, and especially young African American males, as being especially prone to violent crime. Despite some inconsistent research, police stops, searches, and arrests appear to target people of color disproportionately. Arrest seems more likely when victims are white and when the offenses are misdemeanors. In addition, police also appear more likely to use undue force, including fatal force, against people of color.

Chapter 6 focused on prosecution and punishment and pointed to evi-dence of apparent racial/ethnic discrimination in the charging process, in conviction, and in sentencing, with several harsher outcomes in these areas more likely when crime victims are white. Meanwhile, discrimination in sentencing occurs more often in the research evidence for the in/out imprison- onment decision than for sentence length. Sentencing disadvantage is also found more often and sentencing is more severe for young African Ameri-can males than for other combinations of race/ethnicity, age, and gender. Additional troubling research finds that people with darker skin tone and more Afrocentric facial features are more likely to receive harsher sentences.

Chapter 6 also emphasized, as did earlier chapters, that the war against drugs has especially affected African Americans and Latinos, who are more likely than whites to be arrested and incarcerated for drug offenses even though they do not commit drug offenses more often than whites. We also saw that racial discrimination in capital cases is very pronounced regard-ing the race of homicide victims, with capital charges and the death penalty more likely when victims are white than when they are African American. The chapter ended with a discussion of the juvenile justice system, which, much like the adult criminal justice system, exhibits variable effects of race and ethnicity on juvenile justice outcomes, with some but not all studies finding evidence of racial and ethnic bias and discrimination.

All in all, then, this book has portrayed a nation that exhibits a dis-maying continuing dilemma—to borrow from Myrdal's (1944) famous phrase—when it comes to race, ethnicity, and crime. If people of color commit serious conventional crime at higher rates than whites, they do so because they live in a nation filled with racial bias, racial discrimina-tion, and racial inequality, and because many live in neighborhoods with conditions that create criminality. These same factors contribute to their higher rates of crime victimization, which whites' exaggerated fear of victimization by African Americans overlooks.

This continuing dilemma is also reflected in racialized news media coverage of crime, in America's deep racial divisions in views about crime and criminal justice, and in research that reveals racial prejudice as a basis for whites' support for the death penalty and other punishment of criminals. And it is seen throughout the criminal justice system, where there is ample evidence of racial/ethnic bias and discrimination in policing, prosecution, and sentencing. Even if this pattern derives from largely implicit racial bias rather than the Jim Crow racism of the past, it remains unacceptable in a society that aspires to "liberty and justice for all."

All of these problems mean that our nation must do everything possible to achieve a more just criminal justice system and a more just society. The next section sketches policies and strategies that, if adopted and adequately funded and implemented, would help greatly to achieve racial justice both in our society and in our criminal justice process. Much fuller discussion of these policies and strategies may be found elsewhere, but the discussion here will at least point to directions America should follow to establish a more racially just society.

WHAT THE NATION CAN DO

It would be wonderful if we could wave a magic wand and eliminate racial prejudice, racial discrimination, and racial inequality. But this is real life, not Hogwarts Castle nor the Land of Oz, and these scourges of American society are not about to vanish no matter how much we might wish them to disappear. People of color will thus continue to be more likely to live in poverty or near-poverty and in communities with physical and social conditions conducive to crime and victimization, and the criminal justice system will continue to exhibit implicit racial bias and racial discrimination that produce higher incarceration rates for people of color.

This is admittedly a pessimistic outlook, but it is also realistic. At the same time, there is much cause for optimism, because a realistic outlook recognizes that there is still much our nation could do to address the structural causes of higher crime and victimization rates for people of color and to address the many racial inequalities besetting our criminal justice system. Unfortunately, our nation has shown little interest over the decades in addressing these problems, thanks in large part to persistent racial biases and to punitive views about crime that lead politicians and many citizens to have little concern for these problems. Fortunately, much theory and research point to many various measures that would greatly help to address the structural causes of crime and to reduce racial inequality in criminal justice, assuming these measures were adequately funded and implemented. In an optimistic spirit, this section outlines several of these measures.

Addressing the Causes of Crime

Even though racial prejudice and inequality are not about to disappear overnight, there are many steps the nation, states, and/or cities could take, if they wanted to, that hold great promise for addressing the structural roots of crime and thus for reducing the disproportionate involvement of people of color in serious conventional crime. Interested readers are invited to read more complete discussion of these strategies elsewhere (Currie 2013; Rocque, Welsh, and Raine 2012; Weisburd, Farrington, and Gill 2016; Welsh, Braga, and Sullivan 2014; Welsh and Farrington 2012).

Poverty and Neighborhood Conditions

A first set of strategies involves efforts to address the structural causes of crime such as poverty and related neighborhood conditions. This form of crime prevention is called **community prevention**. These strategies include the following:

- Increase public expenditures for job training and other strategies to improve employment prospects for the poor
- Expand government aid to help lift people out of poverty, similar to what most Western democracies other than the United States offer their poor

- End racial segregation in housing, which contributes to the higher crime and victimization rates of African Americans
- Reduce urban neighborhood dilapidation and other physical conditions conducive to crime and victimization
- Increase programming such as youth recreation programs and parental involvement in school efforts to strengthen the social integration of urban neighborhoods
- Establish and expand adult mentoring programs for at-risk youth

Families and Schools

Criminologists recognize that it is absolutely crucial to improve family functioning and the quality of education so that at-risk children will be less likely to commit antisocial behavior and, as they grow older, delinquency and crime. This form of crime prevention is called **developmental prevention**. Specific policies that would help prevent crime by strengthening families and improving schools include the following:

- Establish and expand early childhood intervention programs for at-risk children and their families; these programs, which include home visits by nurses or other professionals and parenting training, are be highly effective in preventing antisocial behavior and in improving children's life outcomes as they age
- Provide affordable and high-quality day care for parents who need it, similar to what most Western democracies other than the United States provide
- Greatly increase funding and other efforts to improve schools in low-income urban and rural areas
- Provide better health and nutrition services for families before and after children's birth, as health problems in infancy and early childhood can impair cognitive and neurological development and in turn generate antisocial behavior

Opportunities for Crime and Victimization

Chapters 3 and 4 emphasized that crime and victimization are more likely when certain opportunities present themselves. Accordingly, many strategies to reduce these opportunities appear to be effective. This form of crime prevention is called **situational prevention**. These situational strategies include the following:

- Install better lighting and closed-circuit television cameras in public places
- Expand neighborhood watch groups
- Expand community policing and directed police activity in crime hot spots, while preserving civil liberties
- Expand *focused deterrence* strategies that target specific gang members and other chronic offenders, while preserving civil liberties
- Increase gun safety efforts, including technologies to reduce the use of handguns by unauthorized persons and strategies to keep handguns from potentially dangerous offenders

Reforming Criminal Justice

Many scholars and other observers have proposed various reforms to improve the quality of criminal justice in America, and in particular to prevent injustices based on race/ethnicity and social class. Just as mass incarceration has negatively affected people of color disproportionately, so will any criminal justice reforms help them disproportionately. Interested readers are again invited to read more complete discussion of these reforms elsewhere (Berman and Fox 2016; Cullen 2013; Davis 2017; Ghandnoosh 2015; Jonson and Cullen 2015; Tonry 2012; Travis, Western, and Redburn 2014; Weisburd, Farrington, and Gill 2016; Yoffe 2017). Specific criminal justice strategies include the following:

- Establish and expand racial-bias education and training programs for police, prosecutors, judges, and other criminal justice professionals
- Consider decriminalizing many illegal drugs, and, at a minimum, target minority drug offenders only in proportion to their rate of drug offenses
- Eliminate the death penalty, which is racially discriminatory, arbitrary, and ineffective in reducing homicide
- Improve and expand legal defense for indigent defendants and regulate plea bargaining to reduce guilty pleas by innocent defendants

- Eliminate mandatory minimum sentencing and shorten maximum sentences more generally
- Expand use of noncustodial sentences (*community corrections*) for property offenders and other nonviolent offenders
- Expand and improve substance abuse, mental health, educational and vocational, and other services for jail and prison inmates
- Improve prisoner reentry programs that help released prisoners adjust to society

WHAT YOU CAN DO

The 1960s Southern civil rights movement showed that ordinary people could change the nation. College students sat in at segregated lunch counters, and thousands of people of all ages and backgrounds marched and protested for an end to legal segregation. Thousands were also arrested and jailed, others were beaten, and some were murdered. Through all their heroic efforts, the movement ended legal segregation and began to change racial attitudes throughout America.

Although much racial inequality still exists today, the nation is also a much better place today thanks to the civil rights movement. Other social movements of the contemporary era have been beneficial as well, including the Chicano civil rights movement, the environmental movement, the gay rights movement, and the women's movement. These and other movements have improved the lives of countless Americans, just as social movements in other nations have improved the lives of untold numbers of people around the world (Meyer 2015; Staggenborg 2016).

Unfortunately, before Black Lives Matter emerged just a few years ago, there had not yet been a criminal justice reform movement in the contemporary era. Scholars, journalists, and other writers have certainly called attention to the many racial inequalities surrounding crime and criminal justice, but a sustained criminal justice reform movement has been lacking. Black Lives Matter became an important voice when it emerged, but there is still so much more that other people can do to address the many issues raised in this book.

Readers of this book could begin talking to their peers, family members, and coworkers about the issues discussed herein. They could meet with criminal justice officials and politicians and other policymakers to urge them to undertake the kinds of reforms outlined in the preceding pages. They could organize rallies, protest marches, and other nonviolent efforts to call attention to racial disparities in crime and justice. Ordinary people can make a difference through all these efforts and more.

Anthropologist Margaret Mead once observed, "Never doubt that a small group of thoughtful, committed citizens can change the world; indeed, it's the only thing that ever has" (Lutkehaus 2008:261).

Eleanor Roosevelt (1943:83) wrote, "I know that we will be the sufferers if we let great wrongs occur without exerting ourselves to correct them."

Dr. Martin Luther King, Jr., reminded us, "Injustice anywhere is a threat to justice everywhere" (Rieder 2013:138) and "Every step toward the goal of justice requires sacrifice, suffering, and struggle; the tireless exertions and passionate concern of dedicated individuals" (King 1958/2010:191).

Nineteenth-century education reformer Horace Mann told college students, "Be ashamed to die until you have won some victory for humanity" (Mann 1868:575).

And Rosa Parks, who refused to move to the back of a bus, later said, "I knew someone had to take the first step and I made up my mind not to move" (http://rosaparksfacts.com/rosa-parks-quotes/).

It is time to take that first step to confront racial disparities in crime and justice. It is time for ordinary people to once again change the nation. Thanks to scholars and activists, we know what can and must be done to eliminate the appalling American dilemma that this book has discussed. It is time once again to win another victory for humanity.

SUMMARY

1. This book informed readers about the overrepresentation of people of color in the criminal justice system, racial bias in news media crime stories, racial divisions in public opinion about crime and

justice, racial differences in crime and victimization, and racial disparities in the criminal justice system.

2. Many steps could be taken to reduce racial disparities in crime and criminal justice. Measures to reduce racial disparities in crime and victimization fall under the areas of community prevention, developmental prevention, and situational prevention.

3. Reforms to achieve justice and reduce excesses in the criminal justice system would disproportionately help people of color, given their disproportionate involvement in criminal justice.

4. The Southern civil rights movement ended legal segregation and reminds us that ordinary people can change the nation. A strengthened criminal justice reform movement is needed to reduce racial disparities in crime and justice.

KEY TERMS

community prevention. Efforts to prevent crime and victimization by addressing their structural causes

developmental prevention. Efforts to prevent crime and victimization by improving families and schools to reduce the likelihood that at-risk children will turn to antisocial behavior and delinquency

situational prevention. Efforts to prevent crime and victimization by reducing the opportunities for these events to occur

REFERENCES

Berman, Greg, and Aubrey Fox. 2016. *Trial and Error in Criminal Justice Reform: Learning from Failure.* Lanham, MD: Rowman & Littlefield.

Cullen, Francis T. 2013. "Rehabilitation: Beyond Nothing Works." *Crime and Justice* 42(1):299–376.

Currie, Elliott. 2013. *Crime and Punishment in America.* New York: Metropolitan Books.

Davis, Angela J. 2017. *Policing the Black Man: Arrest, Prosecution, and Imprisonment.* New York: Pantheon Books.

Ghandnoosh, Nazgol. 2015. *Black Lives Matter: Eliminating Racial Inequity in the Criminal Justice System*. Washington, DC: Sentencing Project.

Jonson, Cheryl Lero, and Francis T. Cullen. 2015. "Prisoner Reentry Programs." *Crime and Justice* 44(1):517–75.

King, Martin Luther, Jr. 1958//2010. *Stride Toward Freedom: The Montgomery Story*. Boston: Beacon Press.

————. 1968. *Where Do We Go from Here: Chaos or Community?* Boston: Beacon Press.

Lutkehaus, Nancy C. 2008. *Margaret Mead: The Making of an American Icon*. Princeton, NJ: Princeton University Press.

Mann, Mary Tyler Peabody, ed. 1868. *Life and Works of Horace Mann*. Boston: Walker, Fuller.

Meyer, David S. 2015. *The Politics of Protest: Social Movements in America*. New York: Oxford University Press.

Myrdal, Gunnar. 1944. *An American Dilemma: The Negro Problem and Modern Democracy*. New York: Harper & Brothers.

Rieder, Jonathan. 2013. *Gospel of Freedom: Martin Luther King, Jr.'s Letter from Birmingham Jail and the Struggle That Changed a Nation*. New York: Bloomsbury Press.

Rocque, Michael, Brandon C. Welsh, and Adrian Raine. 2012. "Biosocial Criminology and Modern Crime Prevention." *Journal of Criminal Justice* 40(4):306–12.

Roosevelt, Eleanor. 1943. *My Day: The Best of Eleanor Roosevelt's Acclaimed Newspaper Columns, 1936–1962*. New York: Da Capo Press.

Staggenborg, Suzanne. 2016. *Social Movements*. New York: Oxford University Press.

Tonry, Michael. 2012. *Punishing Race: A Continuing American Dilemma*. New York: Oxford University Press.

Travis, Jeremy, Bruce Western, and Steve Redburn, eds. 2014. *The Growth of Incarceration in the United States: Exploring Causes and Consequences*. Washington, DC: National Academies Press.

Weisburd, David, David P. Farrington, and Charlotte Gill, eds. 2016. *What Works in Crime Prevention and Rehabilitation: Lessons from Systematic Reviews*. New York: Springer.

Welsh, Brandon C., Anthony A. Braga, and Christopher J. Sullivan. 2014. "Serious Youth Violence and Innovative Prevention: On the Emerging Link Between Public Health and Criminology." *Justice Quarterly* 31(3): 500–523.

Welsh, Brandon C., and David P. Farrington, eds. 2012. *The Oxford Handbook of Crime Prevention*. New York: Oxford University Press.

Yoffe, Emily. 2017. "Innocence Is Irrelevant." *Atlantic* September. https://www.theatlantic.com/magazine/archive/2017/09/innocence-is-irrelevant/534171/

INDEX

Note: Page references followed by a "*t*" indicate table; "*f*" indicate figure.

Printed in the USA/Agawam, MA
July 28, 2021

778630.002